EDUCATING FOR ACTION

STRATEGIES TO IGNITE SOCIAL JUSTICE

JASON DEL GANDIO
ANTHONY J. NOCELLA II

new society
PUBLISHERS

Cover design by Diane McIntosh.
All images ©iStock (Matches: mariosFM77, Protest: BenThomasPhoto)

Printed in Canada. First printing June 2014.

New Society Publishers acknowledges the financial support of the Government of
Canada through the Canada Book Fund (CBF) for our publishing activities.

Inquiries regarding requests to reprint all or part of *Educating for Action*
should be addressed to New Society Publishers at the address below.

To order directly from the publishers, please call toll-free
(North America) 1-800-567-6772, or order online at www.newsociety.com

Any other inquiries can be directed by mail to:

New Society Publishers
P.O. Box 189, Gabriola Island, BC V0R 1X0, Canada
(250) 247-9737

LIBRARY AND ARCHIVES CANADA CATALOGUING IN PUBLICATION

Educating for action : strategies to ignite social justice / Jason
del Gandio, Anthony J. Nocella II.

Includes bibliographical references and index.
Issued in print and electronic formats.
ISBN 978-0-86571-776-3 (pbk.).—ISBN 978-1-55092-570-8 (ebook)

1. Social action—United States.   2. Social justice—United States.
3. Social movements—United States.   4. Social change—United States.
5. Peace.   I. Nocella, Anthony J., editor   II. Del Gandio, Jason, editor

HN65.E36 2014   361.20973   C2014-902144-5
                                                     C2014-902145-3

New Society Publishers' mission is to publish books that contribute in fundamental
ways to building an ecologically sustainable and just society, and to do so with the
least possible impact on the environment, in a manner that models this vision. We
are committed to doing this not just through education, but through action. The
interior pages of our bound books are printed on Forest Stewardship Council®-
registered acid-free paper that is 100% post-consumer recycled (100% old growth
forest-free), processed chlorine-free, and printed with vegetable-based, low-VOC
inks, with covers produced using FSC®-registered stock. New Society also works to
reduce its carbon footprint, and purchases carbon offsets based on an annual audit
to ensure a carbon neutral footprint. For further information, or to browse our
full list of books and purchase securely, visit our website at: www.newsociety.com

*This book is dedicated to
all the people—past, present, and future—who
put their bodies on the line in the service of peace and justice.
It is these people we most admire, and it is these people
who make this world a better place.*

Contents

Part 4: Social Networks

Part 5: Institutional Change

Acknowledgments

JASON AND ANTHONY WOULD LIKE TO THANK THEIR FAMILIES and friends for their lifetime of support, guidance, and encouragement. They may not always agree with us, but that is the beauty of discussion and debate—expressing differences in the service of deeper understanding and mutual transformation. It is such a value that has laid the groundwork for our own sense of justice and rebellion—cutting against the grain, standing up for our beliefs, and fighting for what we believe to be righteous and just. Jason and Anthony would like to also thank all the contributors to this volume; without them this would not have been possible: Anniessa Antar, Larry Albert Butz, Melissa Chiprin, James Generic, Jenny Grubbs, Joshua Ryan Holst, Joy James, Michael Loadenthal, Dara Lovitz, Peter McLaren, Alisha Page, Jeanette Russell, Kim Socha, Rita Verma, Drew Robert Winter, and Aaron Zellhoefer. And lastly, Jason and Anthony would like to thank everyone at New Society Publishers.

Reading Peace Education

JOY JAMES ▇▇▇▇

▇▇ EDITORS JASON DEL GANDIO AND ANTHONY J. NOCELLA II, along with volume contributors, present *Educating for Action: Strategies to Ignite Social Justice* as an engaging and instructive manual for social justice, suitable for both students and teachers, as well as for larger activist communities. This organizing manifesto goes beyond elementary ideas, as it offers original essays from scholars and activists concerned with a plethora of issues—LGBTQ, human and animal rights, disability rights, hip-hop, environmentalism, prison abolition, feminism, and more.

Educating for Action confronts painful injustices that may overwhelm some while being denied by others. Inspired by social justice, the authors—and we—work as "wounded healers," laborers for beauty and justice through activism fueled by injuries in an injurious world. Wounded healers turn trauma into acts of service to end violence and exploitation. Activism, even when countered and co-opted by corporations and governments, facilitates a creative consciousness that enables healing, sustainability, and freedom.

Present-day activists are indebted to their predecessors. Social justice has always reflected and been enabled by an intergenerational agenda, one made more relevant by the chapters in this volume grappling with poverty, racial and sexual violence, imprisonment, war, and the rights of animals and the natural world.

Current preoccupations with the mundane or extraordinary circumstances of our lives appear to leave little time to devote to justice and activism. Global capitalism's unregulated predations; technology's invasive envelopment of jobs, medicine, food, and personal relations; crises in human rights and natural environments; and, of course, war and mass destruction—all distract from closer reflections on what is sacred and just, and within our reach. But we should always remember that material and spiritual poverty coexist with the imaginative and courageous desire to publicly address inequities and violations that are critiqued in *Educating for action*.

This volume marries realism with wisdom and energizing analyses for the greater good. The authors understand the necessity to balance expectation and acceptance, aggression and restraint, narcissism and compassion. The sacrifices of past, present, and future activists are reflected in the resolve of this volume.

Educating for action confronts the seismic shifts predicted by the movements of previous decades. In half a century, we've seen deep-reaching and troubling changes. At an economic level, we have seen the increase of concentrated wealth and poverty. At a political level, we have seen corporations alter legal protections guaranteed by the Fourteenth Amendment, to grant corporations "political personhood" before the law. We have also watched the recoding (rather than abolishing) of slavery in terms of the "prison industrial complex"— the United States, supposedly the greatest democracy on Earth, leads the world in imprisonment, thus enabling brutality and misery to become profitable. If nothing else, this demonstrates an unwillingness and/or inability to shed the lifelong entanglement of the US with captivity and white supremacy. We should recognize, too, the expansion of state police powers. Today, through the PATRIOT Act, presidential signing statements, extraordinary rendition, and collusion between government and private industry, the "warfare state" merges domestic and foreign policy and challenges our very identities as citizens of a republic controlled by a democratic mass.

It is common for people to be both enthralled by *and* suspicious of activists. But let us recognize that activists are sorely needed in this time of injustice and inequality. We should also make a cautionary observation: our age of branding, sound bites, and viral communication makes it easy for political avatars to claim to be doing the work of social transformation when, in fact, they are false heroes dressed in the trappings of racial, class, and educational privileges. We must be on guard and distinguish between the trickery of such avatars and those activists who are truly dedicated to just struggles.

We must also distinguish between individual acts of kindness and conscience and the need for larger systemic change. In Harper Lee's famed novel *To Kill a Mockingbird*, the ethical protagonist Atticus Finch worked against racism and injustice but, ultimately, failed to overcome the wider racist structures. This resulted from a failure to truly critique those structures, largely due to Atticus's white privilege within structural patriarchy and racism. The all-too-common scenario in which the white leader has agency that benefits from the labors or suffering of the "lesser" colored followers reveals racial hierarchy even among politically progressive constituents. Historically, the trauma and rebellions of the racially disenfranchised (think of the Abolitionist and Civil Rights movements, for instance) opened pathways to greater democracy (this is true even for those who reject the reality of black suffering). Reflect, for a moment, on the following sacrifices: the political imprisonment of 1963 Freedom Riders and Student Nonviolent Coordinating Committee activists; Dr. Martin Luther King, Jr.'s Letter from Birmingham Jail and eventual assassination; the lost bodies of four young girls in a bombed Birmingham church; and the trauma of women civil rights activists who survived beatings that turned into sexual assaults. The lives of these people—and many others of varying movements and causes—enable the activists of today to fight and struggle. The unsettling nuances of "race relations" were addressed by the Students for a Democratic Society's Port Huron Statement approximately half a century ago: "The national heritage of racial discrimination via slavery has been a part of America since Christopher Columbus's advent on the new continent...keep this as a background when trying to understand why racism stands as such a steadfast pillar in the culture and custom of the country." In other words, history matters.

Many readers of this volume will be situated in an academic setting—the classroom, the dorm room, the library, the campus rally. Academia can be approached as an important site for addressing social justice. Its "community engagement" and "diversity programs" seek to offset and manage crises disproportionately borne by the poor and disenfranchised. Yet this delivery system of access to elite educational enclaves does not level the playing field because it does not challenge and indict institutional power. The academic setting *is* important, but organizing *beyond academia* is the lifeline to social justice. We need efforts that are independent from the state- and corporate-funded mandates of public or private institutions. We must realize that outside the academy's privileged view, *basic survival* is the foremost concern of activists working among the most forgotten—prisoners, runaway teens, the homeless, the hungry, the domestically abused and assaulted. It is up to all of us who believe that "good enough" is no longer good enough to call out this absence of wellbeing. In doing so, we make the case that tyranny and suffering are no longer accepted and that collective love and compassion are necessary.

Lastly, we must keep in mind that the pursuits of freedom and justice live on forever. Past movements and previous struggles may have become stardust, but they leave trails and traditions that newer generations can pick up and follow. The actions expressed in *Educating for action* contribute to that stardust of confrontation, negotiation, and sacrifice, thus expanding our ability to pursue peace and justice.

Teaching Peace

PETER MCLAREN

IN AN AGE OF ENDLESS WAR, WHEN HISTORY IS IN PERPETUAL mourning, groaning under the burden of class oppression, peace is a necessary practice. In a world redolent of George Orwell's novel *1984*, where war is peace and peace is war, we need to reengage in teaching peace with ontological clarity and a renewed commitment to strategize for social change. Peace education does not guarantee that peace will be achieved, but without peace education we are permanently exiled from victory.

In a world of consumption, saturated with generalized inauthenticity and baptized in the ideology of commonsensical cynicism, in which war is an ever-present contingency for which we must forever be prepared, a deep skepticism should be cultivated toward "official" peace initiatives as mere stagecraft. Governmental gestures of peace often involve encrypted reminders that being a peacemaker today is increasingly reduced to merely acting like a peacemaker while inciting war. Today Oceania is at war with Eurasia. Yesterday *we* were at war with Eurasia. Tomorrow we will be at war with Eastasia. No, we were never at war with Eurasia; our enemy has always been Eastasia. And so on, as Big Brother attempts to channel the aggression of the "proles" toward the imaginary Other and foster mindless group cohesion. That is because today, more than ever, peacemaking is parasitic on the notion of the just war.

But is war ever really just? Christopher Hedges does well to invoke the wisdom of the 15th-century thinker Erasmus on this issue:

> There are no good wars. There are no just wars. As Erasmus wrote, "there is nothing more wicked, more disastrous, more widely destructive, more deeply tenacious, more loathsome" than war. "Whoever heard of a hundred thousand animals rushing together to butcher each other, as men do everywhere?" Erasmus asked. But war, he knew, was very useful to the power elite. War permitted the powerful, in the name of national security and by fostering a culture of fear, to effortlessly strip the citizen of his or her rights. A declaration of war ensures that "all the affairs of the State are at the mercy of the appetites of a few," Erasmus wrote.[1]

Peace is a word that rarely punctuates today's endless forecasts of future wars and the pervasive ambience of political flattery that has infected politics across the United States. It is ominously absent in the lexicon of those in power, such as those who are leading the ascendancy of the transnationalist capitalist class, pitching the economic nostrums of neoliberalism, and facilitating the ruthless dictatorship of the financial markets over 99 percent of humanity. Those menacing the future by financial speculation, wholly unconnected to any genuinely economically productive activity, or by trampling human rights under the banner of national security, rarely or seriously consider peace to be a viable option to the rewards and riches of war. This is certainly true for those who advocate "humanitarian intervention" by US military or economic imperialism. Or for those who preselect targets for weekly drone assassinations, forwarding the information to an overworked military pilot operating a joystick in a clamshell hangar near Las Vegas, waiting for a "kill shot" 7,000 miles away in a remote tribal village in Afghanistan.

I want to pause here and say something about the drones because we are going to be hearing a lot from them in the years to come. Be forewarned.

The high-pitched whirr coming from the shark-grey fuselage of the Predator drone is part of the everyday background noise at Kandahar Airfield in Afghanistan. Seconds after the drone pilots at Kandahar receive the kill list from the pilot at Creech Air Force Base in Nevada, they unleash their machines. Bathed in the Afghan sun, they look in the distance like golden eagles that have pushed off from the arm of a Berkutchi-falconer on the steppes of the Tien Shan mountains, gliding effortlessly toward an unsuspecting prey. Once the drone returns successfully, the pilots at Kandahar can relax and, before the next mission, kick around a ball at the soccer pitch, chat with the private-security contractors cruising in their new SUVs, visit a frozen-yogurt outlet, or chomp down on a grilled steak sandwich at TGI Friday's.

After interviewing Oz, a middle-aged Royal Air Force Reaper pilot based at Creech who has flown three tours of duty in the Tornado, Bob Blackhurst reports the following:

> About four percent of US UAV [Unmanned Aerial Vehicle] operators have developed post-traumatic stress disorder, which some have attributed to the fact that powerful cameras show close-up footage of the targets of drone strikes after they have been killed.
>
> "The cameras are good," Oz says. "A Hellfire missile does have significant effects on the human body, and you should get to see that. If you can't accept it, you are in the wrong job. But the weirdest thing for me—with my background [as a fast-jet pilot]—is the concept of getting up in the morning, driving my kids to school and killing people. That does take a bit of getting used to. For the young guys or the newer guys, that can be an eye-opener."[2]

An eye-opener, indeed. Decades ago, it was impossible to think that the remote control airplanes we played with in parks and empty lots would one day be transformed into devices designed to assassinate foreign nationals (or even US citizens), and which, intentionally or unintentionally, wreak havoc on innocent victims who happen to be in the vicinity. Did we ever think that one day we could purchase a birthday gift for a 12-year-old, a "plane kit" that resembles a 4-Channel Predator-Style Reaper UAV Drone RC, for $139.98? Or the (considerably cheaper) armed RQ-1 Predator Unmanned Aerial Vehicle? Both "toys," easily findable online, have been reviewed with biting sarcasm on the Internet by critics of the Obama administration's targeted killing program. I include but one of my favorite examples:

> The coolest detail[s] about this toy are the small body fragments you can litter around your target area following a drone missile strike on a wedding party. THEN (this is where the real fun begins) you circle back in an hour and fire MORE missiles at the people rescuing survivors and mourning the dead! Sure if another country did such a thing we'd decry it as heinous terrorism, but when good ol' Uncle Sam's finger is on the joystick, you can bet that we call what we hit our target, no matter what.[3]

And if your child isn't too keen on drones, then you could purchase her or him a video game, like Manhunt, that attempts to bring out and nurture your child's "homicidal tendencies." Or the game Resident Evil, where you are able to gouge, saw, and hack into oblivion victims (mostly black) who have turned into zombies. Nowadays, after mass shootings like Columbine and Newton, it is frighteningly possible to imagine a child plaintively asking his or her father, "Daddy, what happens if we are not at war with anyone when I turn 18? How will I get to demonstrate my skills and go after all those evil people like the ones Uncle Johnny or Uncle Bobby killed in Iraq and Afghanistan?"

This may sound far-fetched, but I'm not so sure. And it may seem like a harsh indictment, but, again, I am not so sure. Don't we live in a culture that funds the possibility of such conversations? Isn't our cultural landscape saturated with violence, everything from video games and Hollywood to the glorification of war and guns?

The nature-nurture debate obviously surrounds the causes of war. For example, is war linked to Sigmund Freud's primordial unconscious psyche, or rather to Karl Marx's analysis of capitalist social relations? Such issues will most likely never be resolved completely. But we do know that the "human being" is unquestionably a potential agent of violence in almost every environment—history tells us so. However, we also know that human beings are less likely to commit violence when their basic needs are met satisfactorily (e.g., food, shelter, healthcare, transportation, confirmation, love).

Never before has it been as urgent to introduce peace education to the world's classrooms. And while it is politically prudent to begin with the understanding that official history is written by the winners, we must remember that sometimes the winners like to act like sore losers, demanding that more citizens be detained, more immigrants be turned back at the border, more human rights diminished, and more countries "saved" by the US military. Despite the political toxicity that the "US brand" has undergone over this past decade, Euro-Americans still like to believe that they are entitled to initiate "humanitarian" military and economic interventions into other sovereign states because they set the moral standards of the rest of the world. But the following world rankings call this moral entitlement into question.

A recent report by the United Nation's Children's Fund, entitled *Child Well-Being in Rich Countries*, compiled information taken in the final two years of the last decade (2009–2010). The report revealed a staggering level of child poverty in the "developed" world, with the standards of living in the United States ranking near the bottom on all metrics. Those metrics included material wellbeing, education, health and safety, behaviors and risks, and housing and environment. The US and Great Britain, two of the world's wealthiest nations and unarguably the most war-aggressive countries of all the western states, fall into the lowest ranking for something as seemingly simple as preventing infant deaths.

This is telling, not just for the rankings, but for how we think about "peace." It is a misnomer to think that peace education is mainly or only about ending military conflict and the death and destruction that inevitably are associated with it. Peace education is rightfully directed at social, political, economic, and educational injustices found throughout society. As this handbook reveals, economic inequality, war and the military industrial complex, nonhuman animals and the environment, rape and sexual assault, sweatshops and modern-day slavery, are all struggles engaged by peace educators, often at great risk to their personal safety and livelihood.

Educating for action, edited by two seasoned and respected scholar-activists, constitutes a powerful volume of hands-on strategies for peace. It is a courageous book, aimed at constructing a new society free from oppression and injustice. The history of cruelty does not dictate the future. It can be challenged by peacemakers, such as those represented in this book, who possess the latent necessities for transforming the world. The strategies and tactics contained in this magnificent volume form a unity of theory and practice that can transform the present and the future.

INTRODUCTION

Peace as a Political Force

JASON DEL GANDIO AND ANTHONY J. NOCELLA II

> *There is no way to peace; there is only peace.*
> — MAHATMA GANDHI

> *If you want to make peace, you don't talk
> to your friends. You talk to your enemies.*
> — DESMOND TUTU

> *Peace does not mean an absence of conflicts; differences
> will always be there. Peace means solving these differences
> through peaceful means; through dialogue, education,
> knowledge; and through humane ways.*
> — DALAI LAMA XIV

> *Peace is preferable to war. But it's not an absolute
> value, and so we always ask, "What kind of peace?"*
> — NOAM CHOMSKY

> *Peace is a very complicated concept.
> When the lion gobbles up the lamb and
> wipes his lips, then there's peace.
> Well, I ain't for that peace at all.*
> — ABBIE HOFFMAN

> *There can be no real peace without justice.
> And without resistance there will be no justice.*
> — ARUNDHATI ROY

Peace through Opposition, Conflict, and Struggle

This book is about changing the world through peace. By "peace" we do *not* mean standing around in a circle, holding hands, and expressing our affection for one another. That has its time and place. But we understand peace as a political force for social justice and progressive social change. We must actively work to attain that peace, and that involves opposition, conflict, and struggle. These words usually conjure up negative associations, as if "opposition, conflict, and struggle" are antithetical to "peace." But that's not true. As Dr. Martin Luther King, Jr., once said, "Freedom is never voluntarily given by the oppressor; it must be demanded by the oppressed."[1] In other words, activists and social movements begin with opposition. If there were no opposition, then your desired changes would already exist. That leads to conflict—different people have different views and opinions about what kind of world to live in. You must then struggle to create the world that you envision. That can involve everything from one-on-one conversations to massive demonstrations and protests.

This might make some people doubt themselves. Do I really want to put myself out there like that? Do I want to invite opposition, conflict, and struggle? Do I want to step forward and fight, or would I rather sit back and relax? Such apprehension and doubt are natural. We usually seek the path of least resistance, and for good reason—it makes our lives easier. But that does not get us a better world. Social justice does not happen on its own. There are people, institutions, and systems that are hell-bent on maintaining the status quo. That usually means maintaining—and often expanding—their own power while simultaneously disempowering others. Oppression, marginalization, domination, cruelty, coercion, and individual and systemic violence are real. People, as well as animals and nature, are brutalized on a daily basis. That suffering is neither natural nor inherent. Instead, it is a product of our current world. But the world is up for grabs; it's not on lockdown, and it's not set in stone. Each and every one of us has the right to fight for the world that we want to live in. The question thus becomes: what kind of world do you want?

The Ills of the World

We all know the world is plagued by problems. But it's sometimes important to face those problems head-on—to consciously acknowledge them so you know what you're dealing with. The brief list below is not intended to depress people. Instead, it is about testing your own sense of injustice. After reading this list, do you want to recoil and turn a blind eye? Or, do you want to do something about it?

Economic Inequality

There are approximately 300 million people in the United States. Approximately 46 million of them live at or below the poverty line— e.g., $11,484 for a one-person household, $14,657 for a two-person household, and $17,959 for a three-person household. That means that more than one out of seven people live in poverty.[2] This number could be drastically higher if the "official" poverty lines better reflected actual living conditions. A more honest poverty line for a three-person household (two caregivers and a child) would be a figure closer to $25,000 rather than $18,000. This would more accurately reflect the number of people struggling economically.

By contrast, the average salary in 2009 for an American CEO was 263 times that of the average American worker. So if the average worker made $50,000, that means the average CEO made $13,150,000—that's more than 13 *million dollars*. This ratio is actually lower than in recent years because of the economic recession. In 2007, one year before the Great Recession, a CEO was earning 364 times more than a worker. By contrast, the pay ratio in 1980 was only 40 to 1, and in the mid-1970s, it was 30 to 1.[3] And as of 2007, the richest one percent of the US population owned 34.3 percent of the nation's private wealth (stocks, bonds, property), while the richest 10 percent owned 71 percent of the wealth. But on the other end, the poorest 40 percent of the population owned only one percent of the wealth. Worldwide, 10 percent of the population owns 85 percent of the global wealth.[4]

This economic inequality must be put into perspective. It's not just about money, but rather what that money allows you to do. Having money allows you to eat *nutritional* food, live in a *safe* house and *safe* neighborhood, attain *reliable* transportation, earn a *good* education, receive *quality* healthcare, and make different and, presumably, *better* choices in life. Money also allows you to influence society. For instance, the 2012 presidential and congressional campaigns cost over four billion dollars.[5] Most of that money came from the wealthiest donors. It's very unlikely that a politician will pass laws that inhibit those wealthy donors from earning a profit, even if those laws would benefit the vast majority of (less wealthy) citizens. If this is true, then economic inequality directly affects our political system. In general, the gap between the rich and poor boils down to *quality of life*, *personal opportunity*, and *political power*.

War and the Military-Industrial Complex

The United States has more than 700 military bases worldwide.[6] Its military budget is close to 700 billion dollars every year, accounting for approximately 40 percent of the *world's* total defense budget.[7] Its current nuclear arsenal contains over 5,000 warheads. While this is a far cry from the peak of 31,000 warheads in 1967, it is still enough to bomb the world many times over.[8] It is the first country to develop nuclear weapons and, at the time of this writing, the only country to use nuclear weapons (during World War II). Although the United States often portrays itself as a country of peace, it is perpetually engaged in military conflict of some sort. Here is an abbreviated list of military engagements of the 20th century: World War I and World War II; the Cold War (late 1940s–early 1990s); the Korean War; the Vietnam War; invasion of Grenada (1983); invasion of Panama

(1989); the Gulf War (1991); air strikes into Bosnia (1994–1995); and air strikes into Kosovo (1999). The 21st century then began with "the war on terror," which involved invasions and occupation of Afghanistan (2001) and Iraq (2003), Guantanamo Bay, torture of detainees, and unmanned drone strikes in Pakistan.

Nonhuman Animals and the Environment

Twenty-five million animals are used every year for the researching and testing of cosmetic and household products. Such tests are conducted not only on mice, but also on dogs, rabbits, and chimpanzees.[9] Scientists, military personnel, and medical and veterinarian students conduct experiments on goats, sheep, and numerous other animals. Such experiments involve operations on both deceased *and* living animals, the latter of which might receive no pain medication in order to test stress levels.

Ninety thousand cows and calves are killed every 24 hours in the United States for food consumption. Another 14,000 chickens are killed every minute. Overall, approximately 10 billion food animals (not including marine animals) are killed each year in the US.[10] Much of this food production revolves around factory farming, which is both inhumane and unsustainable.[11] Factory farms neglect and abuse animals and force them into undersized cages filled with their own excrement, severely restricting natural and necessary movement. These unsanitary conditions expose humans to increased possibility of disease and illness: e.g., an estimated 89 percent of US beef patties contain traces of E. coli; approximately 650,000 Americans are sickened by Salmonella-tainted eggs each year; and more than 5,000 people contract food poisoning each year, the primary source of which is contaminated chicken flesh.

Factory farms also devastate the environment. According to the Food and Agriculture Organization of the United Nations, animal agriculture is responsible for 18 percent of human-induced greenhouse gas emissions. This occurs because the production of eggs, milk, and meat involves the production of grain to feed the animals, the production of fertilizer to maintain the soil, and the use of water, gas, and electricity to run operations and transport animals and goods.

Ninety percent of US forests have been cleared over the last 400 years. An area of rainforest the size of a football field is cut down every second. And 56,000 square miles of total forest are lost every year. Worldwide, as of 2008, there were 405 "dead zones"—large areas of ocean in which nothing can live due to fertilizer runoff and sewage dumping in coastal areas.[12] Statistically speaking, each person in the United States generates about 4.6 pounds of trash every day, and 80 percent of what Americans throw away is recyclable.[13]

Rape and Sexual Assault

An alleged rape case has grabbed the national spotlight at the time of this writing. In Steubenville, Ohio, two high school football players have been convicted of raping a 16-year-old female while she was passed out from alcohol. The overall story is unbelievably disturbing and unfortunately commonplace. The two boys filmed themselves talking about the girl, essentially laughing about "raping a dead woman." Many of their friends can be seen in the video or heard off-camera laughing along, all of which was used as evidence against the two boys. This is a small but disturbing glimpse into America's rape culture: high school kids are raised in a culture that sees the female body as a sexual *object* void of human agency; women are literally seen as nonhuman, mere playthings for male sexual pleasure; American manhood and masculinity are defined, in part, through the domination and dehumanization of women and femininity. This cultural context increases the possibility of rape and sexual assault.

The Steubenville case may seem like an isolated incident, but it's not. The Rape, Abuse & Incest National Network, in referencing the US Department of Justice's National Crime Victimization Survey (2006–2010), states that an average of 207,754 victims (age 12 or older) are sexually assaulted each year. That translates into a sexual assault every two minutes. Approximately 44 percent of victims are under the age of 18, and about 80 percent are under the age of 30.

Approximately two-thirds of assaults are committed by someone known to the victim, and about 38 percent of rapists are a friend or acquaintance. Sexual assault is one of the most underreported crimes, with about 54 percent of sexual assaults being left unreported to the police.[14]

Sweatshops and Modern-Day Slavery

Most people have heard of sweatshops. But very few realize the prevalence or brutality of sweatshops. It is safe to say that the large majority of products bought in the United States are made in sweatshops somewhere around the world—footwear, clothing, furniture, toys, video games, auto parts, cell phones, computers. International corporations take advantage of the low labor standards that exist in other countries. Companies "outsource" the manufacturing to plants in China, Sri Lanka, or Honduras, for instance, where goods can be produced at a cheaper cost, allowing corporations to reap greater profits. But why shouldn't the labor standards of US workers apply to *all* workers worldwide? In fact, why can't there be agreed-upon global standards that benefit all workers, regardless of country, race, gender, age, or industry? Does a national border diminish one's right to a fair wage and safe work environment? Does it diminish one's humanity? Do workers in poor countries deserve *fewer* rights and *worse* treatment?

Some people might argue that these other countries have lower economic standards and that workers can therefore be paid lower and, presumably, comparable wages. But this is not true. Almost 75 percent of the retail price of a garment is pure profit for the manufacturer and retailer. Sweatshop workers earn as little as 25 to 50 percent of what they need to provide for basic nutrition, shelter, energy, clothing, education, and transportation. In order to meet the basic nutritional needs of their families, sweatshop workers spend from 50 to 75 percent of their income on food, leaving little money for other necessary expenses. Not only are workers paid less than a living wage, they are often subject to verbal and even physical abuse. Most sweatshop laborers work much longer than eight hours a day, and are given few, if any, breaks, including bathroom breaks. They can even be cheated out of wages altogether.[15]

Slavery is another form of extreme exploitation. We all know of America's horrid history of slavery. But slavery still occurs today, constituting a 32-billion-dollar industry.[16] That figure informs us about the purpose and motivation of slavery: profit. Contemporary slavery can manifest itself in different ways, usually through confinement, servitude, forced labor, and, most commonly, through human trafficking. A typical scenario might involve an individual agreeing to travel to another country on the promise of a job. Once there, the individual is held captive, essentially forced to work for free. The person has no way to contact others, is physically threatened, and can be told that attempting to escape will result in the punishment (and even death) of loved ones back home. All told, approximately 27 million people are held captive in modern-day slavery across the world, thousands of whom are trafficked into US borders annually.[17]

Fighting for Justice: A Social Movement Tradition

The world is filled with grim realities of racism, sexism, classism, ableism, homophobia, and transphobia; of climate change, speciesism, and environmental destruction; of war, imperialism, colonialism, and dictatorialism; of job discrimination, worker exploitation, and child labor; and of abuse, neglect, and random violence. But all is not lost, as good people rise every day to fight for social justice. Activists and social movements play integral roles in correcting social ills. Below is a partial list of some of the more significant social movements throughout US history. As you'll see, there is a long tradition of people fighting for social change.

- **Abolitionist movement** (1830s–1870s): Sought to end legalized segregation and slavery in the United States.
- **Women's Suffrage movement** (mid/late 1800s–1920): Suffrage means "the right to vote." This movement is also referred to as first-wave feminism.
- **US Labor movement** (began in early 1800s with formation of the

first unions, matured into full-blown movement by late 1800s/ early 1900s): Sought unionization, safer working conditions, the 40-hour work week, an end to child labor, and a minimum wage. This movement was also international in that many workers understood the international aspect of capitalism and the shared experience of workers across the world.

ALL STRUGGLES ARE INTERCONNECTED

- **Civil Rights movement** (early/mid 1950s–mid/late 1960s or early 1970s): Sought equal rights for African Americans, focused on ending legalized segregation and ensuring the right to vote.
- **Black Power movement** (mid/late 1960s–mid-1970s): An extension of the Civil Rights movement. People became frustrated with the slow progression of legislation and decided to take direct action. The movement promoted a positive black identity, an embrace of one's African heritage, and the upliftment of the black community.
- **American Indian movement** (late 1960s–today): Focuses on reclaiming its stolen land, honoring its heritage, and attaining tribal sovereignty. Began with concerns of poverty, high unemployment, inadequate housing, and disintegration of American Indian culture.
- **Era of 1960s Radicalism** (mid-1960s–mid-1970s): Involved many different movements—the Anti-Vietnam War movement, the Student movement, the Free Speech movement, the Psychedelic movement—and cultural revolution (e.g., free love, drug experimentation, rock and roll music, different forms of spirituality, hippies, and Yippies).
- **Women's Liberation movement** (early 1970s–1980s): Sought to liberate women from oppressive male dominance; to discuss and advance women's sexual pleasure; to grant women the right to choose abortion; to give women the freedom to have careers and to enter politics; to make women equal to men in every phase

of life and society; to allow women to live their own lives. Often characterized as second-wave feminism.

- **Gay Liberation movement** (late 1960s–early 1980s): Sought to grant visibility to gay, lesbian, bisexual, and transgendered people; wanted the right to live out of the closet and to be accepted by society; sought to end discrimination of sexual orientation in all aspects of life and society. Is often marked by the Stonewall Riots of 1969 in New York City.

- **Pro-Choice movement** (late 1960s–present): Developed most poignantly around the 1973 landmark case of Roe v. Wade that legalized abortion in America.

- **Anti-Nuclear Proliferation movement** (began in late 1960s, became an organized movement in 1980s): This was at the height of the Cold War and the threat of nuclear annihilation. Sought to end nuclear proliferation and even the use of nuclear energy (for electricity, for instance).

- **Identity Politics** (began to emerge in 1980s, continued through late 1990s; still in existence, but not as controversial nowadays): Not necessarily a fully organized movement, but includes a confluence of people, groups, organizations, and ideas about the politics of personal and cultural identity. Is related to such issues as multiculturalism, affirmative action, and political correctness. Is still in effect, but has become more of an accepted understanding toward issues of cultural appreciation, diversity, and identity construction.

- **AIDS/HIV Activist movement** (early 1980s–mid-1990s; still in existence, but not as prominent since AIDS/HIV has received more institutional attention): Emerged in the early 1980s when AIDS (Acquired Immune Deficiency Syndrome) started to become a major pandemic. At the time, the US government was ignoring the disease and the population it was most affecting, gay men.

- **Animal Rights movement** (began in mid-1970s and has gained more traction ever since): Seeks to end the philosophical and even legal distinction between human and nonhuman animals. This may involve greater protection of animals (in nature and in the home), the promotion of vegetarianism and/or veganism, putting an end to animal testing and animal products like leather and fur, and reforming or abolishing zoos or the use of animals for sport and entertainment.

- **Global Justice movement** (mid-1990s–early/mid-2000s): Also known as the Anti- or Alter-globalization movement. Was a cross-continental movement that involved a plethora of smaller issues and movements. Is rightfully understood as a "movement of movements." At its base, it sought to reform (if not totally end) corporate control of politics and society, global capitalism, and use of sweatshop labor. Also promoted greater respect for the relationships between social systems (such as capitalism) and indigenous populations and the natural environment.

- **The Anti-Iraq War movement** (early/mid-2000s): Was at its peak just before and after the start of the Iraq War (March 2003). Major protests occurred, and there were international days of action. Entire city areas were shut down through coordinated direct action. On February 15, 2003, approximately 30 million people across the world protested the impending war.

- **Contemporary Gay Rights movement** (current): Fights for full acceptance and legal rights of people who identity as lesbian, gay, bisexual, transgendered, and queer (LGBTQ). This might involve same-sex marriage, hospital visitation rights for same-sex couples, healthcare protections for transgender and gender-nonconforming people, the legal right to foster and adopt children, anti-bullying policies in schools, more inclusive curriculum, and the US military's "Don't ask, don't tell" policy (repealed in 2011).

- **Immigrant Rights movement** (throughout the 2000s; still current): Major protests and marches occurred in the mid- to late 2000s, with smaller ones occurring before and after. Generally speaking, this movement seeks to create an easier pathway for people to become US citizens and to provide greater benefits to illegal immigrants. Also fights against the xenophobia of anti-immigration policy.

- **Climate Justice movement** (current): Focuses on climate change and global warming. Often targets corporate pollution and government policies that allow corporations to pollute. It advocates for alternative forms of energy and consumption (e.g., sustainable farming practices, alternative forms of fuel, recycling, use of mass transit). In many ways it is an extension of the Environmental movement, which began in the late 1960s/early 1970s and continues today.
- **Occupy movement** (2011): Occupy formed in September 2011 and centered around two major issues: economic inequality and the lack of political accountability. The peak of Occupy lasted only a few months, but its style of protest (occupation of public space) and its radical approach (immediate reformation of the economic and political system) makes it one of the most significant American social movements of recent times.

After reading this list, it becomes obvious that every right, liberty, and freedom that we hold dear has come by way of a social movement. There is no part of our lives that has not been affected by the collective action of activists and organizers working for change: voting rights, civil rights, immigrant rights, human rights, labor regulations, housing regulations, anti-dumping laws, consumer protections, workplace safety, minimum wage, broader and more inclusive college curriculum, procreation and safe sex, anti-discrimination laws, free speech, environmental awareness and appreciation, the ending of wars and genocide, the curbing of nuclear proliferation, and the fight for everyday equality and respect. There's no doubt about it—social movements are thriving contributors to world history.

SOCIAL MOVEMENTS DRIVE THE PROGRESSION OF HISTORY

Overview of Book

This book is written for people who are incensed by injustice and inspired by social movements. It is intended to help beginning activists become *better* activists. To that end, we have collected essays by seasoned activists working in a variety of fields. We are not claiming that this book can teach you everything, but it will get you started on the right path.

The book is organized into five sections containing 10 chapters. The sections are: "Starting with Me," "Working with Others," "Getting into the Streets," "Social Networks," and "Institutional Change."

Section One: Starting with Me

You have to be clear about your own wants, needs, skills, and abilities before you start reaching out to others. This section helps you do that. In chapter one, "Personal Lifestyle," Larry Albert Butz discusses how you can use your everyday life as a source of activism. The products you buy, the clothes you wear, the stores you shop at, and even the language you use can affect the world. If that is true, then you want to critically reflect on your own life and learn to make choices that manifest the change you want to see. In chapter two, "Communication and Rhetoric," Jason Del Gandio addresses the common critique that activists have "no clear message." Del Gandio provides guidelines for improving your speaking, writing, message construction, and persuasive appeal. It is not just what you say, but also how you say it, that moves people to action.

Section Two: Working with Others

Activism involves working with other people. That may seem easy, but it's actually very challenging. How do you facilitate a meeting? How do you make group decisions without alienating people? How do you negotiate different opinions? How do you act more democratically? How do you work together in a cohesive and productive manner? Joshua Ryan Holst's chapter three, "Participation and Democracy" covers the history of democracy, examples of different forms of democracy, and how to use direct democracy. By the end of the chapter you will know how to democratically participate in everything from electoral processes to street demonstrations. In chapter four, "Transformative Justice aand Conflict Transformation," the authors, Anthony J. Nocella II, Melissa Chiprin, Anniessa Antar and Alisha Page outline different ways to deal with conflict. Most people think of conflict as something negative and to be avoided. But as the authors demonstrate, conflict is part of human experience. We should thus learn to deal with it in a transformative manner that brings about greater peace for everyone involved.

Section Three: Getting into the Streets

This section provides examples of and strategies for moving people to action. How do you get people involved? What kinds of events and activities should you create? Are some actions better than others? In chapter five, "Organizing Your Community," Drew Robert Winter outlines strategies for organizing isolated individuals into a unified group committed to running a public campaign: designate a problem, contact likely allies, propose a solution, and persuade people to act. Organizing is obviously more difficult than this, but Winter provides concrete steps for getting the job done. Chapter six, "Activist Guidelines and Case Studies" is a collaboration among four authors, with each author outlining a specific case study of an activist project. Jason Del Gandio uses his experience with Occupy Philly's media working group to outline steps for facilitating public organizing meetings. James Generic provides an overview of the Wooden Shoe bookstore, which is an all-volunteer, collectively run, and financially viable store based on anarchist principles. Aaron Zellhoefer discusses how the group Minnesota United for All Families used a strategy of engaged conversation to successfully oppose an amendment outlawing same-sex marriage. And Anthony J. Nocella II discusses his experience with Save the Kids, a grassroots organization that uses hip-hop activism and the principles of transformative justice to keep kids out of incarceration.

Section Four: Social Networks

Broad and diverse networks make social change possible. No one does it alone; it always involves numerous people working toward a common goal. This section focuses on conference-building and virtual connections. In chapter seven, "The Politics of Planning: Conference Organizing as an Act of Resistance," Jenny Grubbs and

Michael Loadenthal provide a step-by-step outline of how to organize an activist conference. As they clearly explain, such events are necessary for building solidarity, sharing ideas, strategizing for long-term change, and simply meeting like-minded people. That last one is more important than you think—you begin to form bonds of friendship through your activism, which helps sustain your drive for social change. Jeanette Russell walks us through the world of wireless connection with chapter eight, "Social Media and Online Organizing." As the title suggests, Russell discusses how the Internet and social media can be used to spread messages and expand activist networks. She covers everything from tools (Facebook, Twitter, and websites) to strategies (crafting Internet-based sound bites).

Section Five: Institutional Change

This last section addresses the importance of working within the system in order to change the system. There are far too many systems and institutions to cover here. We thus focus on two that have broad appeal: law and education. Dara Lovitz addresses the importance of the legal system in chapter nine, "The Laws and Lawyers of Social Change." She explains why lawyers are needed in the battle for social justice, outlines some historical landmark court cases that have changed our world for the better, and discusses different law careers that activists might pursue. And lastly, chapter ten, "The Courage to Teach Critically: Anti-Oppression and Pro-Justice Dialogues in the Classroom," discusses both the problems and promises of the educational system. Critical pedagogue Rita Verma argues that the classroom should be approached as an opportunity for personal growth, political conversation, and anti-oppression work. The classroom is a place to not only think about, but to actually *do*, social change. This is true for both students and teachers.

Closing Remarks

We have gone to great lengths to provide an accessible and inspiring how-to handbook. We have therefore included a list of helpful books, organizations, and websites at the very end. We hope that these various sources cross-pollinate in your pursuit of peace and justice. As the famous historian Howard Zinn once said, "You can't be neutral on a moving train."[18] The world is already moving, and it is up to you to move it in the right direction. Action does not guarantee success, but inaction guarantees failure. We hope that you can use this book on your journey toward a better world.

PART 1

STARTING WITH ME

Personal Lifestyle

LARRY ALBERT BUTZ

What I have to do is see...
that I do not lend myself to
the wrong which I condemn.
— HENRY DAVID THOREAU

THIS CHAPTER FOCUSES ON HOW TO USE YOUR DAILY ACTIVI-
ties to create a more just and ethical world. The chapter stresses the
benefits of using your everyday life as a means to your politics. While
I do on occasion make passing reference to the limitations of this
technique, I definitely believe that "everyday activism" is a great place
to start—it's personal, political, and effective.

What Is Personal Lifestyle?

The word "lifestyle" is sometimes used pejoratively when talking
about systemic social change. Someone might say, for instance, that
boycotting Walmart due to its business practices is ineffective for
challenging corporate greed and malpractice. Such a criticism has a
point—one person's boycott will not make or break Walmart's multi-
billion-dollar operation. But one person *can* help mobilize others
to do the same. People influence people, and if you can get enough
people to boycott, then Walmart will be forced to change. Personal
boycotts also reflect the famous quote attributed to Gandhi, which

states that you must "be the change you wish to see."[1] In other words, we should withdraw our participation from systems that we seek to change and, conversely, enact the changes that we believe in.

Cultural critics and historians argue that, since 1915, when consumerism began reaching new heights in the United States, Americans have tied their sense of freedom to product consumption. As people increasingly connected their identities to commodities (i.e., products and goods that are bought and sold), the word "lifestyle," which originally referred to the choices people made that made them uniquely themselves, began to be used as a way to refer to the changing notion of identity as it merged with commodity relations. Lifestyle now refers to our daily practices of eating *particular* foods, wearing *particular* clothes, driving *particular* cars, living in *particular* homes, surrounding ourselves with *particular* brands, and in general consuming a plethora of *particular* commodities.

Commonly, the phrase "personal lifestyle" conjures up notions of your own habits and practices, as if your personal life does not affect others. But that's a misnomer, since our lives are interconnected in a multitude of ways. As Dr. Martin Luther King, Jr., once said so eloquently,

> All men [and women] are interdependent. Every nation is an heir of a vast treasury of ideas and labor to which both the living and the dead of all nations have contributed. Whether we realize it or not, each of us lives eternally "in the red." We are everlasting debtors to known and unknown men and women. When we arise in the morning, we go into the bathroom where we reach for a sponge which is provided for us by a Pacific Islander. We reach for soap that is created for us by a European. Then at the table we drink coffee that is provided for us by a South American, or tea by a Chinese, or cocoa by a West African. Before we leave for our jobs we are already beholden to more than half the world.
>
> In a real sense, all life is interrelated. The agony of the poor impoverishes the rich; the betterment of the poor enriches the rich. We are inevitably our brother's keeper because we

are our brother's brother. Whatever affects one directly affects all indirectly.[2]

Dr. King's quote summarizes the point of lifestyle politics: our lives are interconnected, and one's own privilege and power is often enabled by the oppression and disempowerment of others. If this is true, then I must find a way to live my life that does more good than harm.

Think of your own daily activities. There are very few that do not affect people, nonhuman animals, the environment, the climate. Your mode of transportation has some impact on the environment, the clothes you purchase affect factory workers' lives across the world, and the food you eat is of huge ethical importance since agriculture, especially meat production, is a leading contributor to climate change. The point is to recognize that our behaviors are expressions of our values, beliefs, ethics, and worldviews. If you believe in climate justice, then you need to think about what you can do to lessen climate change. If you believe that all creatures are free, sentient beings, then you need to think about the food you eat. If you believe that all workers—regardless of national borders—deserve fair pay and treatment, then you need to think about the products that you buy. These issues boil down to behaviors—what you *do* and the *impact* of that doing.

DR. KING'S use of nonviolent passive resistance was directly influenced by his study of **GANDHI,** who was influenced by the likes of **HENRY DAVID THOREAU, RALPH WALDO EMERSON,** and **LEO TOLSTOY.** And they all believed in using our personal lives to prefigure a **BETTER WORLD.**

This way of acting is usually called *lifestyle activism*. As I said above, this term is sometimes used as an insult, as if using one's personal life as a form of activism is insufficient and thus a less worthy form of activism. I believe a better term is *everyday activism*—the practice of embodying one's activism in everyday activities.

Everyday Activism

Individual behaviors are part of larger social systems—e.g., familial, economic, educational, political, religious, and cultural systems. Due to the nature of our present society, everyday activism can have the biggest impact on the economic rather than the political system.

It is hard to affect the government through everyday activism, for instance. Boycotting Congress, refusing to vote, or ignoring presidential discourse will probably *hurt* your political cause. As the great philosopher and social critic Karl Marx noted in the 1800s, most human relations are actually economic relations. While we have come a long way since Marx, his insight is truer now than ever before—the economy permeates our lives. Everyday activists can use this insight to impact the world.

WHAT CHANGES can you make in your everyday life to have a **POSITIVE IMPACT** on the world? The clothes you wear, the food you eat, the transportation you use, the words you choose are all important for **SOCIAL CHANGE.**

When looking at a product, there are two basic sides to consider: production-side issues and consumption-side issues. Production-side issues involve everything that happens in the creation of the product. This might be, for instance, the environmental impact of mining minerals or harvesting plants; the labor conditions of workers; the pay equality within a company; the treatment of women employees or the benefits package given to LGBTQ employees; the treatment of chickens and cows in the production of eggs and milk; or the amount of pollution generated in the production of oil. Consumption-side issues involve everything that happens in the use and disposal of a product. This might be the release of harmful gases from aerosol products; the cancer-causing agents in antiperspirants; the environmental damage caused by nonrecyclable materials; the pollution caused by driving SUVs; the acid leaked from old batteries; the chemicals that leak into one's body when drinking from plastic bottles; or the health issues associated with fast food consumption. Addressing these issues is rarely straightforward since an economy is a complex system with moving parts. One conscientious action can be easily absorbed by the wider system, and taking action against one chain store might have unintended consequences (hurting workers who might be laid off, for instance). But generally speaking, we can use our basic purchasing power to create some changes, which is the topic of the next section.

Impacts of Purchasing

The key to effective everyday consumer activism is maximizing the positive and minimizing the negative impact of purchases. In terms of maximizing the positive, you can consider what is done with the money that you are spending. Does the company pay its employees well? Does it invest in the community? Does it altruistically contribute to charity? Does it promote "going green"? To maximize the positive impact of your consumerism, try spending your money at worker-run or cooperatively owned businesses, or at the very least, small, family-owned businesses. These businesses tend to be more ethical, worker-friendly, and community-oriented, and far more trustworthy. They might even have social missions like helping the environment or donating a portion of profits to community organizations.

To minimize the negative, you can choose to avoid businesses that, for instance, excessively pollute the environment, violate safety regulations, fund politicians and policies that you oppose, harm wildlife or captive animals, mistreat and/or underpay workers, or support military dictatorships in other countries. It may be difficult at first glance to distinguish between "good" and "bad" companies. I recall reading a story in the early 2000s about a tobacco company that donated 60 million dollars to charity, but then spent 80 million dollars publicizing its gift. If the company were really that conscientious, it could have simply donated *all* of the money to charity. But this is where basic research comes in. For instance, a quick online search for "top 10 unethical companies" turns up more than one million hits. The first hit that shows up in my search is the organization "Action for Our Planet." Its number one unethical company is Monsanto:

> The Missouri-based agricultural company has been named the world's most unethical company. The company leads the world's production of genetically modified foods. Monsanto is infamous for unfairly suing farmers who try to grow foods both ethically and organically. If the lawsuit is not ruled in

Monsanto's favor, they still achieve their desired results as the small-scale farms become bankrupt due to legal costs. The company is also the creator of the highly poisonous herbicide named Roundup (a weed killer). This weed killer is both damaging to ecology as well as humans. A 2008 scientific study found Roundup can cause the death of unborn children.[3]

Factory farms are another example of unethical practices. Obviously, they are a phenomenon or a practice rather than a company. But the same idea applies: avoid them whenever possible. Factory farms are practiced by large-scale agribusiness. They are a major contributor to air and water pollution and a leading cause of climate change. They often exploit migrant labor and undocumented immigrants, brutalize and torture nonhuman animals, and rely on public infrastructure (e.g., highways and water supplies) and government subsidies. Factory farms thus benefit from the public sector for private gain while destroying the collective commons (e.g., land, nature, atmosphere). In contrast, we can and should support small-scale sustainable farms and buy from cooperatives or farmers' markets. This avoids many or even all of those negative effects, while also giving money to people who will invest in local schools, churches, infrastructure, and politicians.

Alternative Markets

Many people, whether they be everyday activists or not, prefer to shop in so-called *alternative markets* that exist at a distance from the mainstream economy. One type of alternative market, the *farmers' market*, is often populated with stalls and stands of small-scale agricultural workers and craft producers who can tell you all you need to know about the product, where it comes from, and how it was produced. In many ways, the food goes from the farm to your table with little distance or disturbance, and you can usually be confident that it's organic, chemical-free, and environmentally friendly.

Food cooperatives (or just food co-ops) are food distribution centers organized by those who actually work at the centers. According to the Neighborhood Food Cooperation Association, co-ops are "based on the values of self-help, self-responsibility, democracy, equality, equity and solidarity. In the tradition of their founders, co-operative members believe in the ethical values of honesty, openness, social responsibility and caring for others."[4] Food co-ops often serve as alternatives to supermarkets, providing connections between the goods on the shelves and the consumers that shop there. While supermarkets are often impersonal and put profit before people, co-ops intentionally foster personal relationships, offer more ethical food choices (locally grown, green-friendly, etc.), and involve group decision-making within the workplace. It is also common for food co-ops to have more specialty items than supermarkets, thus offering more interesting options.

Increasingly popular are the *"really really free market"* events in which people bring things they no longer want or need to give to others for free. People are encouraged to swap, and nothing is allowed to be sold. Some participants bring used items, and some bring things they make for hobbies, which they would like to give away. The idea is that goods actually are consumed based on their value to interested individuals rather than their capitalistic exchange value or profitability. This is similar to *"freecycle"* groups, in which things are cycled around from person to person. Once one person is done with the item, it is passed on to another who needs it. Similar are *"free stores,"* where everything in the store is literally free. Free stores are not very common since it costs money to keep a store open—rent is needed, if nothing else. But the history of free stores dates back to at least the 1960s, and on occasion you can still find one.

Underground markets or *black markets* tend to be unregulated and technically illegal economies that sell goods for cash but function out of the reach of law enforcement. While the reputation for these is fairly bad, such as in dealing in illegal and harmful goods that you could not otherwise buy in the normal market (drugs, guns, stolen items), many people have sought to form underground markets to avoid having to pay sales taxes that would go to support government action to which they are morally opposed. While underground markets often deal in illegal activities and goods, there's nothing stopping people from creating more ethical and politically motivated underground markets.

Labeling

Everyday activists need to be informed about product labeling. At the surface, the labeling of products with "fat-free," "organic," and "chemical-free" statements seems like a great way to navigate the consumer landscape. But labeling is often under-regulated or even unregulated, which enables companies to prey on consumers' good intentions. One example of this is "greenwashing," in which companies market their products as environmentally friendly, although, in actuality, these companies and/or products might be *damaging* the environment.

LABELS are not always **ACCURATE** or honest. Do **RESEARCH** to find out what's **BEHIND** the label.

Below are some common labels. I discuss the reliability of these labels and briefly evaluate the impact that you can make by using these types of products.

Cruelty-free

Cruelty-free labels are meant to indicate that the product has not been tested on animals. Cosmetics and cleaning products are infamous for their cruel and violent tests on rabbits, cats, dogs, rats, and other animals. The cruelty-free label is supposed to enable consumers to avoid products that use animal testing.

But who does this labeling? Unfortunately, cruelty-free labeling is not regulated and is often done by the company that makes the product. It is a kind of honor system in which companies are supposed to "do the right thing." The consequences of lying may be a media firestorm and consumer outrage that hurt profits. But the meaning of the label is very unclear. For instance, some products might have ingredients that were tested on animals, while the final product was not. Other times, the company that does the labeling might not have tested on animals but instead had a third party do the testing. There is simply no guarantee of what is meant by "cruelty-free."

Fortunately, the Coalition for Consumer Information on Cosmetics (CCIC) has started its own labeling initiative to solve this problem, at least for cosmetic products. It is called the Leaping Bunny Program, and works by putting a rabbit label on products that were truly not tested on animals and also by encouraging cosmetics companies to pledge not to test on animals. (Testing on animals for cosmetics in the United States is completely voluntary, whereas in Europe it is actually banned.)

To guarantee that you are buying cruelty-free cosmetics and cleaning products, look for the CCIC label or check if an independent group has verified the product. You can also look up the "compassionate shopping guides" at the websites of People for the Ethical Treatment of Animals and the Humane Society.

Fair Trade

Fair trade labeling is part of a large international social movement intended to make it easier for consumers to support producing communities by buying goods that are environmentally friendly and that offer workers a higher percentage of profits. The motto is that fair trade is good for both producers and consumers. Sometimes this takes the shape of alternative marketplaces, such as the Ten Thousand Villages chain store that sells exclusively fair trade products. You can also find fair-trade-certified products in places like Trader Joe's and Whole Foods grocery stores.

Certification in the United States is very reliable, with groups such as Fair Trade USA, Fair Trade Federation, and Equal Exchange all offering trustworthy labels. These groups tend to have very high standards and genuinely strive to achieve meaningful and lasting change in all fair trade communities. Fair trade chocolate, for instance, is often made by cooperatives that have seen transformations in the standard of living among producers. Coffee villages in Latin America have been able to build schools and hospitals because of well-meaning consumers who are committed to buying more ethical products.

Unfortunately, the fair trade label has been exploited at times. In one case, a major coffeehouse chain used the phrase "fairly traded" to

imply that their coffee was fair trade when it was not. Largely, however, the label initiatives have been very successful, and consumer
demand has been high: Starbucks gets a reasonable percentage of
its coffee from fair-trade-certified producers; Dunkin' Donuts gets
all of its espresso (but not necessarily all of its coffee) from fair trade
producers; and independent coffeehouses offer fair trade brews for
the everyday activist.

A common criticism of fair trade is that it is expensive for producers to get certifications. But fair trade activists work tirelessly to
help workers form cooperatives and get certified. Academics such
as Michigan State University's Paulette Stenzel have shown that fair
trade has helped significantly improve the lives of producers and has
even helped developing nations resist the policies of the International Monetary Fund and the World Bank.[5]

Organic

The US Department of Agriculture's "Organic" label is meant to
guarantee that products and goods are made without artificial fertil-
izers, pesticides, and other toxic chemicals. Because of the demand
by well-meaning consumers, organic products have grown exponen-
tially, taking up a sizable chunk of the market.

Companies can call pretty much anything organic, so you need
to look for the USDA certification. However, the labeling system is
fraught with problems. Even if a product is USDA-certified, it does
not mean the product does not contain heavily synthesized ingredients. In many cases, Organic-certified products have been shown to
contain ingredients that would not be able to get certified as Organic
by the USDA. Also, the USDA is not primarily a consumer organization, but rather a wing of the agriculture industry which self-reg-
ulates. That industry is often criticized for promoting the companies
to which its staff have strong connections. Many critics thus feel
that the USDA cannot be trusted. Finally, "organic" does nothing
to address such issues as greenhouse gas emissions that contribute
to climate change, or land and water degradation that result from

monocropping and excessive use of animal manure (think of factory farms, for instance). While organic might be good for the human body, it is not necessarily good for nonhuman animals or the planet at large. Organic, consequently, is not always a reliable or effective tool for everyday activists concerned about environmental issues.

Shade-grown

"Shade-grown" refers to coffee plants that are grown under a canopy of trees, which is a fairly sustainable practice. Coffee plantations have wreaked havoc on rainforests, which are necessary for biodiversity and fending off climate change. Shade-grown certifications, such as those by Bird Friendly and the Rainforest Alliance, attempt to make sure that growers use sustainable permaculture practices. Companies cannot get certified unless they meet the standards of these nonprofit groups. In general, certified shade-grown practices include minimal amounts of water use, and the minimization of water pollution, soil erosion, deforestation, and negative health impact. At times, the environmental standards of shade-grown-certified products are higher than those for fair trade or USDA Organic, although shade-grown products may be harder to find. Because this certification is not very widespread, the lack of the label on some coffee does not necessarily mean that the standards are not met.

Other Popular Labels

Cage-free: While this indicates that poultry are no longer kept in battery cages the size of single sheets of paper, birds may still be subject to many violent industry practices and may still live in extremely cramped and unhealthy conditions.

Free-range: This guarantees that chickens spend some time outside, but "outside" may be a small balcony or windowed space. This label does not address other cruel treatments of the birds or the chemicals (such as hormones and steroids) that are given to them. And, of course, "free-range" does not address the impact of these chemicals on human health.

Kosher: This refers to food that conforms to Jewish dietary law, which is thought to be limited in helping people make more general/ secular ethical choices.

Halal: This refers to food that conforms to Islamic legal code, which is thought to be limited in helping people make more general/secular ethical choices.

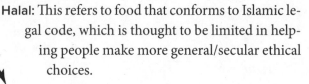

Symbolic Power

Everyday activism is not reducible to direct impact on the economy. This is because we are a symbolic species, meaning that our actions and behaviors communicate meaning to others. Social norms are established when we recognize, collectively, that (1) particular behaviors mean particular things; and (2) those behaviors/meanings are "the normal" way to behave and interpret the world.

Imagine shopping at a supermarket and strolling through the aisles. You will most likely see a lot of meat and meat products— chicken, beef, pork, lamb, fish, hamburgers, hot dogs, crab cakes. This scene is communicating that eating meat is common and normal. We also see lots of milk, eggs, butter, and other dairy products. We can even look at secondary items, such as soup and gravy, which are often made of beef or chicken broth, and gelatin, which is made of animal collagen. All of this implicitly communicates that animals are for human consumption. In fact, this taken-for-granted assumption is so common that many people never even think about the use of animals in the production of food. This is an example of how social norms work to hide themselves—the norms are so taken for granted that we have little impetus to reflect upon them and call them into question.[6]

But this situation can be challenged by everyday activism. You can choose, for instance, to go vegan. In your own life, you will not eat any meat or animal products whatsoever, such as cheese, milk, and butter. While this is a private act, it also has a public component. Your friends, family, work colleagues, and even some strangers will notice your veganism. They will most likely ask you questions, which will lead to discussions about your choices and motivations. When people come to your house, they will notice that you have only animal-free foods. When eating out, you will order not only fresh greens, but meat substitutes and alternative proteins like non-genetically modified whole grains and legumes. Your consumption of these foods implicitly communicates a counter-norm: that animals exist in their own right and we should avoid eating meat.

Everyday activism is applicable to many different issues: wearing only clothes not made in sweatshops; using local credit unions rather than big corporate banks; using mass transit and riding a bicycle rather than driving your own car; using reusable rather than disposable water bottles; recycling plastic, paper, glass, and metal; using the least amount of electricity possible; refusing to shop at particular stores, and not just as a temporary boycott, but as a lifelong commitment. These are not the "normal" choices that most people make. But your choices have a symbolic effect on others, which can spark small but nonetheless significant social change.[7]

Combining Lifestyle with Other Movements

Everyday activism can be effective, but it is most powerful when coupled with larger social movements. For instance, the Black Power movement (BPM) of the 1960s–'70s was an extension of the Civil Rights movement (CRM). The CRM was primarily concerned with legal rights—getting certain laws passed that would enable African Americans to be treated equally to whites. The BPM obviously supported such efforts, but it was also concerned with developing a positive and affirmative black identity—understanding beauty from a black perspective, understanding black history, becoming comfortable with expressing one's "blackness," promoting black art and poetry, creating black businesses in black communities. These issues of everyday activism would not have been nearly as powerful if they had not been connected to the CRM. In many ways, these two movements were the expression of an interconnected struggle—to obtain freedom and equality for African Americans and the acceptance and appreciation of black culture.

The act of veganism mentioned earlier definitely has connections to wider social movements—e.g., animal rights, animal welfare, and animal advocacy. Not every vegan is a self-described activist. But many vegans do develop some form of activist orientation and therefore contribute to social change beyond their own personal lives. As one example, legislatures across the country have been passing bills to basically outlaw the actions of animal liberation activists. In brief, these activists seek to expose the commonplace cruelty of animal-exploiting industries (e.g., food and agriculture, entertainment, fur and leather). Animal liberationists can be, and have been, imprisoned with members of al-Qaeda simply for boycotting animal agriculture, an act which is now illegal under the Animal Enterprise Terrorism Act, passed in 2006. How was such an Orwellian law passed? The pocketbooks of major corporations were being hurt by animal liberationists, and these corporations were able to cajole Congress into passing the bill.[8] While this law is unjust, it does demonstrate the power of combining everyday activism with larger social movements: roughly one percent of the US population is vegan and an even smaller percentage is involved with animal rights and liberation, but these activists were capable of scaring a multi-billion-dollar industry.

From Economic to Interpersonal Concerns

Many of our everyday activities do not involve our economic system, or even our political system. But these activities are still extremely important for social change. Just the way we treat each other in our personal interactions contributes to our shared social world—interpersonal relations, emotional support, compassion, willingness to listen and empathize, and signs of mutual aid and care are part of being an ethical human being.

There are far too many interpersonal issues to address here. But language is one place to start. What kind of language do we use in our everyday lives, and how does that language either oppress or liberate ourselves and others? Feminists have been at the forefront of addressing the relationship between language and everyday activism.[9] They have pointed out that there is a close relationship between our everyday language (e.g., *hu-man*, *chick*, or *the female doctor*) and the ways in which women are generally perceived and treated in society. Similar issues apply to race (the "N word"), gender (*sissy*), sexuality (*That's so gay*), mental and physical abilities (*retarded* and *lame*), and so on.

It would be impossible to cover all the ways in which we can cultivate a more ethical and politically conscientious language. The points below are thus basic entryways to your own strategies. Think especially about the ways in which the following examples interrelate with and speak back to wider economic, legal, political, and even religious discourses.

Change the **LANGUAGE** and you **CHANGE** how people **THINK.** Change how people think and you **INCREASE** the chance of changing their behaviors and **ACTIONS.**

- **Racist and xenophobic language:** This refers to racial slurs, as well as inappropriate comments about someone's religion, heritage, culture, or ancestry. Many activists argue that even when the language is not disparaging, discussing race or ethnicity in certain contexts leads to a coding that may charge social situations with discrimination ("the black police officer" or "Arabs always do X").

- **Homophobic language:** This type of language often equates homosexuality with inferiority, evil, the abject, and/or the unacceptable. Saying something like "That's so gay" implies that people who identify as non-heterosexual are bad, wrong, or less-than. The slur "fag" also brings with it a certain type of violence toward non-heterosexual men. Think about it: Is that word every really used in a positive and affirming way that empowers another person? It's possible, but it's very rare, especially when used by someone who identifies as heterosexual.

- **Transphobic language:** People who do not identify as the biological sex that they were assigned at birth face some of the worst discrimination and violence in the United States today. Different people identify their gender in different ways, and gender and biological sex are not reducible to one another. Someone may be born as a biological female (due to particular chromosomes and sex organs), but that person may not identify as "female." Consequently, referring to this person as *either* "man" *or* "woman" could be offensive since this person identifies as neither. This points to the problems of something seemingly as simple as using "he or she." What about folks who stand outside of this simple binary?

- **Sexist language:** This refers to any language that devalues women and/or the female experience. Although it still occurs, it is less likely nowadays to hear overt sexist language such as "A woman's place is in the home." But there are definitely more implicit examples. When Hilary Clinton ran for the presidency in 2008, people debated if she was feminine *enough* or *too* feminine. But no one ever debated Barack Obama's masculinity (although they *did* debate his "blackness"). It should be noted that men and the male experience can also be targets of sexist language. However, this is far less common given the patriarchal structures of our society.

- **Ableist language:** This refers to language that either expresses a superiority of able-bodied or able-minded people or expresses an inferiority of people whose bodies and minds are not thought to conform to socially normative models. Examples include anything that negatively refers to physical and mental disabilities, such as *idiot, moron, stupid, lame,* and *retarded*.

- **Speciesist language:** Animal advocates often argue that the language we use when referring to nonhuman animals influences how we relate to them. By using the pronoun "it," we imply that nonhuman animals are just objects and do not deserve any of the consideration that a person receives. They also argue that euphemisms such as *meat* instead of *flesh*, or *pork* instead of *pig flesh*, allow us to turn nonhuman animals into mere commodities and distance ourselves from the reality of our consuming them.

Concluding Thoughts

So how do you become an everyday activist? You begin with self-reflection. What do you believe in? What kind of world would you like to create? What do you oppose, what are you for, and why? Now, consider how can you translate this reflection into practice. We all live with some kind of contradiction or gap between what we truly believe and how we actually live. And you can't end war simply by being peaceful to your neighbors. But if you are serious about social change, you must enact that change in your personal life. That is the whole point of everyday activism. Be the change you want to see.

2

Communication and Rhetoric

JASON DEL GANDIO

*Students of rhetorical movements and social protest
understand that words are deeds, that language has a force
and effect in the world. To study the rhetoric of social protest
is to study how symbols—words, signs, images, music, even
bodies—shape our perceptions of reality and invite us to act
accordingly. In this sense, speeches delivered at rallies,
protest marches, letters to the editor, manifestos, image
events on the public screen, and many other rhetorical
practices are types of symbolic action, the reality of
which is very much in evidence all around us.*

—CHARLES E. MORRIS III AND STEPHEN HOWARD BROWNE

Our word is our weapon.

—SUBCOMANDANTE MARCOS

THIS CHAPTER HELPS ACTIVISTS IMPROVE THEIR COMMUNI-cation skills and rhetorical strategies. The two basic skills of speaking and writing are covered in detail. The chapter then outlines various strategies for analyzing audiences, constructing effective messages, creating achievable goals, and understanding how different social situations necessitate certain kinds of communication and rhetoric.

Hopefully, by the end, you will understand how communication and rhetoric are primary tools for changing the world.

A Story of Communication and Rhetoric

You walk through the doors of the local coffee shop and take a look at the bulletin board of flyers. You have seen many of them before. But there is one at the top right-hand corner that grabs your attention. It's not necessarily bigger than the others, but its design, color scheme, and font choices are far more interesting, and its image is eye-popping. You take a closer look and realize that it's an invitation to attend the next organizational meeting for a massive rally that will be occurring in Washington, DC. You decide right then and there to attend the meeting.

You are at the meeting, and you don't really know anyone, so you are quiet and reserved. As the meeting starts, you quickly notice that the facilitator is phenomenal. She is energetic, charismatic, and articulate. She moves through the facilitation process effortlessly. She knows how to field questions and direct the conversation in a productive manner. She is never rattled or frustrated. She even handles the strange, off-the-wall comments with ease. Her facilitation skills are enough to make you come back to the next meeting.

A couple of weeks have passed, and you have become involved with the group. The day of the rally finally arrives, and it is your job to distribute informational pamphlets. You're moving through the massive crowd of 75,000 people. Signs, slogans, banners, chants, flyers, bullhorns, and all kinds of street theater animate the environment. Then, seemingly out of nowhere, you are struck by the oratorical abilities of the speaker on stage. You are too far away to see the person, but his voice, words, and passion grab your attention. A buzz fills the air, and despite all that is occurring around you, *this speech* is most memorable.

The day is just about over, and you are heading back to the bus that will take you home. On the way there, you are stopped by a reporter who wants to ask you a few questions. You are nervous at first, thinking that perhaps she should ask one of the more seasoned organizers. But you then realize that you *are* ready for this. Why? Because you attended a "media teach-in" just two days earlier at the local coffee shop back home. The organizers taught you some of the ins and outs of media relations, helped you create sound bites and talking points, and prepared you for some of the "gotcha questions" that reporters might ask. You then pause for just a moment to gather your thoughts and begin answering the reporter's questions. The interview goes smoothly, and you do a great job. It was easier than you would have thought.

Activism and Communication

As an activist, everything you do involves some form of communication: speaking at rallies, writing letters to representatives, designing posters, creating websites, distributing flyers, soliciting donations, conducting teach-ins, facilitating meetings, organizing protests, doing direct actions, negotiating permits, working with media, sending out emails, and even trying to persuade your "conservative uncle." Improving your ability to communicate therefore improves your ability to change the world.

The people who have the greatest impact are usually the greatest communicators: Frederick Douglass, Sojourner Truth, Mother Jones, Emma Goldman, Mahatma Gandhi, Dr. Martin Luther King, Jr., Malcolm X, Fred Hampton, Ella Baker, Che Guevara, Cesar Chavez, Saul Alinsky, Abbie Hoffman, Subcomandante Marcos, Howard Zinn, bell hooks, Cindy Sheehan, and so on and so on.

Ironically, many activists—even good activists—bypass the importance of communication. Some folks never think about communication, while many others mistakenly assume that facts and information are enough to change the world. These latter folks assume that people just need to be properly informed about the social ills and injustices of the world, that such information alone will transform people's consciences. There is some truth to this— understanding what's wrong in the world *can* motivate people to take action. But facts are not enough since all "facts" are subject to interpretation. When discussing economic inequality, for instance,

I might state that more than 46,000,000 Americans live below the poverty line. Most people reading this book will probably see this figure as an indictment of capitalism and/or the US social system. But many other people will argue that those 46,000,000 people don't work hard enough, that they are lazy freeloaders, that they get what they deserve. I personally believe that this latter interpretation is not only uninformed and misguided, but also cold and morally corrupt. But such indignation is not enough. I must labor over the issue and figure out a way to persuasively express my view. What must I say and/or do to persuade others to change their understanding of poverty? How can I effectively communicate the political and moral complexities of this situation? Should I use statistics, a logical argument, emotional appeals, or personal narratives?

This task arises with every discussion and debate: Is war good or bad? Was the US invasion of Iraq justified? Does the mass media do its job? Should the banks have been bailed out? Is America a meritocracy? Does free trade help or hurt the poor? Is same-sex marriage a civil rights issue? Should humans eat other animals? Should we boycott sweatshop labor? Can corporate greed be reformed? Is pacifism a viable solution to the world's problems?

There are no clear-cut, black-and-white answers to these questions. This highlights the crux of the issue: it is not just *what* you say, but also, and more importantly, *how* you say it. All information— even the most basic, concrete facts—must be *rhetorically packaged*. Activists must *communicatively craft* their thoughts, words, ideas, narratives, emotions, demands, images, and actions. Taking up such a rhetorical attitude maximizes your ability to bring about profound social change.

The word "rhetoric" is usually met with suspicion. That's because rhetoric is often equated with manipulation, dishonesty, deceitfulness, and/or coercion. There are two reasons for this—historical and experiential. Historically speaking, Western culture has had a negative understand-

SOCIAL CHANGE

RHETORIC ⟶ ACTIVISM

ing of rhetoric for the last 2,500 years. The famous Greek philosopher Plato vilified rhetoric, arguing that philosophy discovers and/or creates truth, while rhetoric simply conveys that truth. Rhetoric was thus cast as a derivative of truth: there is the truth, which stands independent of one's interpretation and bias; and then there are different ways to communicate that truth to others, which are often subject to one's personal intentions, prejudices, and political motivations. In this scenario, truth is valued as essential and unchanging, while communication is devalued as arbitrary and relative. Plato's student, Aristotle, tried to rectify rhetoric, arguing that truth is meaningless without the proper means of communication. What good is the truth if one cannot communicate that truth to others? Despite Aristotle's attempts, many, if not most, Western thinkers have maintained a general bias against rhetoric.

In more immediate terms, people's negative understanding of rhetoric is based on their everyday experience. Simply put, people are tired of all the rhetorical games. We live in an age of euphemisms and manufactured deceit. Every politician promises that s/he is the candidate of hope and change, but it all stays the same. Corporations echo gestures of "social responsibility" while they set up sweatshops and destroy the planet. Food companies promote healthy options but never disclose the dirty politics of seed production, factory farming, food monopolies, and genetically modified foods. Marketing and advertising industries sell us luxuries and conveniences by preying on our anxieties and insecurities. The "captains of consciousness" deceive us while the world goes to hell. People understand this manipulation, and that's why they are wary of "rhetoric."

This caution toward rhetoric is understandable but misplaced. The rhetoric of particular people—such as politicians and political pundits—shouldn't be conflated with the overall importance and power of rhetoric. As a basic definition, rhetoric is well-crafted communication that allows you to achieve your personal, social, and/or political goals. Everyone engages in rhetoric all the time; it's an ongoing process that permeates everyday life. But activists must become more conscious of this process; activists must become more strategic about their communication and the effects thereof. Failure to do this inhibits your ability to create social change. You *can* be passionate, engaging, and unwavering *without* being dishonest, deceitful, or corrupt. The trick is to be politically demanding while being *communicatively intelligent* and *rhetorically effective.*

Beginning with Communication

One place to begin is with two basic forms of communication: speaking and writing. At first glance, these may not seem very fun or attractive. Things like wireless technologies and social networks seem more relevant to today's activists. But you cannot create websites, use Twitter, or update online statuses without first knowing how to speak and write. These skills can *always* be improved, and they easily transfer to most, if not all, other activist endeavors.

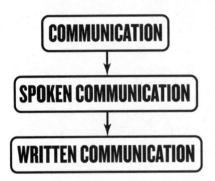

Speaking

Speaking starts with your *delivery*—the overall look and gesturing of your body. This is true whether you are speaking on a stage with a thousand-person audience or you are speaking with a single individual during a face-to-face conversation. Your body is on display, and the audience (of whatever size) watches and responds to that display. Good speakers are in control of their bodies and avoid nervous habits such as tapping feet or fidgeting fingers. Such things distract the audience and can damage your credibility. Good speakers also seem to speak effortlessly. They are comfortable, in control, and their bodies appear natural, as if they have done this a million times. Some people *have* spoken a million times. But most people have spoken only a few times, if at all. Despite these differences, everyone can *look* natural. That's the key to good delivery—you want to look comfortable, confident, natural, and inviting. The following are some basic guidelines for improving your delivery.

- **Articulate yourself as clearly as possible:** Avoid mumbling, speaking under your breath, trailing off at the end of sentences, or under-pronouncing words. Try to articulate each syllable, each word, and each sentence. But don't overdo it, either. Take your time and try to be precise, but also be yourself. Speak as you speak, but be aware of how you sound and how others perceive you. One way to accomplish this is by controlling your *rate of speech*. Some people talk too fast, while others talk too slow. Try to keep the audience in mind, and alter your rate of speech so that others can follow and understand.

- **Adjust your volume:** People cannot be moved and inspired if they cannot hear you. Always speak loudly enough for everyone to hear. If you are in a large (or even small) room, try to speak to the last person in the back row. You want to *project your voice up and out of your body*. This is done by speaking from your diaphragm, which is a little muscle that sits just above your stomach and just below your rib cage. Your diaphragm pushes air up, through, and out, giving you more sound, volume, and resonance. (Doing an online search for "speaking from your diaphragm" will turn up plenty of information and instructions.) Volume is usually not an issue during a one-on-one conversation. But even then, good volume can help your confidence and overall demeanor.

- **Be aware of your facial expressions:** The face is the most visible and expressive part of the body. It is rarely covered by clothing, desks, podiums, lecterns, or crowds of people. Instead, the face is there for all to see. Your facial expressions should therefore match the emotions of your talk; use your facial expressions to enhance and further communicate your message.

- **Maintain eye contact:** Most Western cultures appreciate and respect eye contact. It communicates confidence, poise, control, and honesty. Looking up at the ceiling, down at the floor, or to either side usually communicates the opposite. Eye contact can be very difficult for beginning speakers. It can make you more nervous if you are not prepared for it. But it becomes easier with experience. Try to make and maintain eye contact in a leisurely, comfortable manner. Realize that this is different from *staring* at people. Maintaining natural eye contact makes people feel comfortable. Staring at people is intimidating and awkward. Realize, too, that this is relative to each culture. Many Asian cultures, for instance, interpret direct eye contact as disrespectful; it is more respectful to bow one's head, which demonstrates deference to the other person. There's no way to know the rules of every culture. But you should be aware of the surrounding culture and do your best to adjust. Most people appreciate such attempts.

- **Use your overall bodily movement to communicate:** The entire body is a communicative apparatus. We constantly read and respond to one another's bodies and make interpretations about the "meaning" of what others are doing. The overwhelming majority of gestures are not consciously executed. We usually don't intend a particular meaning with each movement or gesture. But good speakers are aware of their bodies and use their bodies to their advantage. Posture, hand gestures, the sway of your torso, the placement and movement of your legs, and your overall movement can contribute to your message. Know what your body is doing, know what you are trying to communicate, and make sure the two match. But again, *do not overdo it*. You will come off fake and too mechanical. Try to be relaxed and in the moment.
- **Adjust your overall attitude:** Be aware of your overall attitude and orientation. No one likes to be talked down to or yelled at. People also dislike arrogance and/or presumptuousness. Strive for confidence, poise, composure, and spontaneity, but also be humble. Be engaging but not pushy. Be personable but not overbearing. Never be afraid to be angry and enraged, but also realize that you could be mistaken in your beliefs and convictions. Such a balanced attitude can grant you respect.
- **Always rehearse:** Many people think rehearsal is unnecessary. This is a *huge* mistake. Rehearsal helps you improve your delivery, as well as the content and organization of your message. The amount of time spent rehearsing really depends on you and

the situation. Giving a major speech at a rally demands a good amount of rehearsal time, much of which will focus on delivery. Organizing teach-ins and workshops (of whatever size) also demands rehearsal, but the focus is probably on content/information rather than delivery. Whatever the situation may be, try standing up and practicing the presentation. This allows you to assess what works and what doesn't. The rehearsal process often feels awkward because it makes you self-conscious. But that's the whole point—to become more conscious of your speaking abilities. Keep in mind, too, that even a one-on-one conversation can be improved with a little rehearsal. If nothing else, jot down some notes and practice in your head what you will say and how you will say it. This is even more important if you are going on radio or television or into a lobbying session. Think about, craft, and practice *out loud* your talking points.

Writing

The first thing to realize is that writing and speaking are two different forms of communication. Lots of good writing has an oral tone. Slam poetry, for instance, is gritty and fast-paced and intended to be spoken. Subtract the live performance and slam poetry doesn't "read" the same. Slam is thus an oral mode of communication. But most good writing is actually the opposite—it's made to be read silently and not spoken out loud to others. Understanding this distinction enhances the effectiveness of your writing. Craft it for the ear if it's intended to be heard, and craft it for the eye if it's intended to be read. Either choice is fine, but make sure that you are clear on your own intention. One caveat to this is reading your work out loud in order to improve your writing. Even if the writing is intended to be read (rather than heard) by others, listening to your own writing can help your grammar, sentence structure, narrative voice, and flow of thoughts.

Also realize that *reading is labor-intensive*. Reading takes more time and effort than listening. Such effort conflicts with our sound-bite culture. We are accustomed to emails, texts, tweets, status updates, online postings, and three-word news scrolls. People now need a good reason to read past a few pages (or even a few lines). If this is true, then activists need to hone their writing skills and come up with interesting topics and angles. People want to be captured by both the form and content. They want an enjoyable read that addresses new and refreshing issues. Doing this attracts people to your politics, which is the whole point.

It is good practice to *regularly think about your writing*. This keeps you in the groove of writing even when you are not physically doing it. Some of the greatest thoughts occur at unexpected times, such as sitting on the train, walking the streets, or staring out the window. Those fleeting thoughts can help the structure of your essay, create a great one-liner, or even help you solve a social or political problem. You should capture these thoughts by writing them down whenever possible. Have a thought? Jot it down. This can be done in a notebook or with a smartphone. You can also use Post-its or scrap paper that can then be placed in a drawer or folder. Some of these notes lead to extended ideas and insights; most of them won't. Either way, you are thinking about and thus *improving* your writing.

Now it's time to begin the actual writing process. This includes selecting a topic to write about; finding a unique angle; creating a thesis; writing a rough draft; editing and proofreading; seeking feedback; and finalizing the piece.

1. **Select a topic:** What do you want to write about—war, poverty, homophobia, revolution, nonviolent civil disobedience, presidential politics, the past, the present, the future? There are a million possible topics. Whatever you choose, make sure that you find it personally meaningful and interesting. What moves *you* to action?

2. **Find an angle:** You need to develop an original angle or perspective on the topic. There are a million ways to cover every topic. But what's *your* angle? Finding that angle can be difficult, particularly for beginning writers. But the more time you spend doing your activism, the more experience you will have to draw from. Choose a topic, think about your personal experience, and then develop a unique angle.

3. **Create a thesis:** An angle is a unique approach to the topic, while a thesis is a single statement or idea that is fleshed out and supported. In other words, craft your angle into a clear thesis. Begin by stating the thesis in one complete sentence. This provides a guideline for your thoughts and ideas. Realize that this process isn't for everyone. I personally do *not* write this way. Instead, I begin with some faint idea, and my thesis emerges after a considerable amount of writing, deleting, and rewriting. But a thesis always emerges. After I find that thesis, I flesh it out into a larger work. You need to discover your own writing process. But almost every writer develops and then follows through with a thesis. The thesis is the main point of your piece; it is the reason why you are writing and others are reading.

4. **Write a rough draft:** Rough drafts are essential. Very few people are capable of creating a piece of writing that is worthy of public circulation in a single draft . Can it happen? Sure. Does it happen often? Not really. Single drafts often look just like what they are— hastily written thoughts that are confusing and nonsensical.

5. **Edit and proofread:** Everyone makes mistakes, and that's fine. But those mistakes shouldn't be presented to the world. Misspellings, grammatical errors, and non-sensible ideas hinder your ability to change the world. The average person assumes that bad writing equals bad political views. That's not necessarily true, but it's instructive. Putting forth your best effort increases your chances of changing the world. We don't always have time to create well-written, beautifully crafted essays. Deadlines are real. But every good writer reads through the piece *at least a few times*, making corrections here and there. Here are some basic things to look for as you edit and proofread: spelling, grammar, organizational structure, flow of thoughts, accessibility for your audience, narrative voice, overall style, and emotional/intellectual/rhetorical impact.

6. **Seek feedback:** Getting feedback can help with editing and proofreading, but, more importantly, it gives you an audience prior to public circulation. Getting professional feedback is not always possible. Very few of us have editors on hand. But you can

get feedback in other ways: ask friends for advice; partner up with others to read one another's work; start or join a writing group; or put your work online and invite comments. You can also solicit specific feedback by explaining to people what you are looking for. Should the person look for basic grammar? The way the idea unfolds? The unique angle? The organization?

7. **Finalize the piece:** The final draft can be produced for very different purposes—for example, an official magazine publication, a blog entry on your own website, an informational pamphlet for your organization, or a zine. Whatever the end purpose, realize that you are interacting with the public. You have worked on this piece of writing, and you are now placing it into the world. Maybe it will make an impact and maybe it won't. Either way, you have attempted to communicate with others. And that's what counts— taking the risk and putting it out there.

Moving On to Rhetoric

Communication and rhetoric obviously go hand-in-hand. But whereas communication focuses on delivery and presentation, rhetoric focuses on content and strategy. You can always improve your rhetorical preparation by asking yourself five basic questions:

1. What is my **message**?
2. Who is my **audience**?
3. What is my **rhetorical strategy**?
4. What is my **goal**?
5. What is the **situation**?

Here is an example of how it might work:

1. **Message:** The government should bail out students rather than banks.
2. **Audience:** College students (many of whom are *not* politically active).
3. **Rhetorical strategy:** Use both statistics and personal narratives about the increasing costs of college tuition, student loan debt, and the 2008 bank bailouts.

4. **Goal:** The primary goal is to get more students involved with the current campaign for student debt relief. This goal is supported by two smaller goals—getting students to sign a petition and to sign up for the next organizational meeting.

5. **Situation:** A teach-in on campus, lasting one-and-a-half hours.

I refer to this group of five questions as a *rhetorical package*. The purpose is to outline your approach and give you a strategic plan of action. You do not have to always begin with "message" and end with "situation." It is very natural to move back and forth among the different questions as you prepare your package. But all the pieces should fit together in a sensible manner by the time you are finished with your preparation.

Looking at the above rhetorical package from the bottom up, the *situation* is specified as a teach-in that lasts a specific amount of time. That amount of time is important—it structures how much you can say and do. Make sure that you do not try to do too much. You have to account for introductions, latecomers, interruptions, questions and answers, etc. Such issues should be accounted for *before* the actual teach-in. It's good practice to incorporate some additional leeway time. If it's a 90-minute event, then create a 75-minute presentation, giving yourself an extra 15 minutes for unexpected issues, extended talk, etc. Also, when working with a group, specify who will do what. Designate roles in advance. This ensures that everyone has ample time to prepare, and it avoids confusion the day of.

The *goal* is also specified—to get students involved in the current campaign. This goal is different from simply informing the audience. Inspiring people to action is different from just inducing reflection. There are also two mini-goals: to get attendees to sign a petition and to get them to sign up for the next meeting. These smaller goals are "icebreakers" for folks who are not yet politically committed. You cannot expect everyone to jump on board right away. Most people need to be eased into the world of activism. These two mini-goals help move them in that direction. But even these two smaller goals need some thought and preparation. First, make sure you have enough petitions at the teach-in. Second, make sure that you have a date, time, and location for the next meeting—this increases the chance that people will actually attend. And third, make sure you pass around a sign-in sheet that collects names, phone numbers, and email addresses. This information can be used for future organizing purposes.

A *rhetorical strategy* is needed to help facilitate these action-oriented goals. The basic information of the teach-in is made up of facts and statistics. But personal narratives are also being used, and these narratives are just as important as the hard facts. Stories allow us to connect with one another in ways that statistics do not. These particular stories and their storytellers will focus on student debt and economic hardships. To be effective, the storytellers must work on their stories *before* the teach-in. Bad stories are confusing, hard to follow, and in general, *a huge turnoff*. Good stories, on the other hand, allow us to see the world through the eyes of the storyteller. This provokes empathy, which is extremely important for understanding the plight of other people. These stories can then be contrasted with the stories of the millionaire bankers that got bailed out. That dramatic contrast is the *centerpiece* of the rhetorical strategy.

But there must also be time for group discussion. Relaying the basic information (such as facts and statistics) places the audience in a passive position—they sit and listen. The narratives are emotional and personal, which helps to draw in the audience. The discussion is the most interactive part because it's participatory. The more people discuss, the more they feel comfortable and part of the teach-in. This could inspire them to become more politically active, which is your goal as you nudge them toward signing the petition, coming to the next meeting, and hopefully joining the campaign.

Realize, too, that facts/statistics and narratives are only two possible rhetorical strategies. Here is a general list of possible strategies:

- Provide straightforward, *logical arguments* (for example: if you oppose A, and A is similar to B, then you should also oppose B).
- Show a *documentary*, either in part or in whole.
- Show *personal video footage* of actual events that you've experienced.

- Juxtapose *shocking images* (videos, photographs, artwork).
- Organize a *political-poetry night*.
- Play *music* at the beginning and the end of your event.
- Play a political song that highlights your main message/goal and then collectively discuss its *lyrics*.
- Use thought-provoking *analogies and metaphors*.
- Use official *government reports* to support your arguments (the US Census, for example).
- Highlight *mass media and/or government hypocrisies*, biases, and inconsistencies.
- Use *language that stresses* community, togetherness, and collective sensibility.
- Highlight and draw upon *collective struggles and identities*, such as class, race, sexuality, gender, and religion.
- Connect radical ideas, causes, and social movements to *traditionally accepted ideas* of free speech, equality, civil rights, peace, and self-determination.
- Generate *audience participation* through role-playing, group exercises, and group collaboration.
- As a group, create *hypothetical solutions to actual problems*, and then ask, "What's stopping us?"
- Communicate with passion and urgency; speak to *people's desires* and imaginations.
- Use street theater and *political performance* (including costumes, scripts, and blocking/stage directions).
- Use *humor and satire*.
- Organize a *panel of experts* and/or "big names" to speak about the issue.

Realize that your strategy must be adapted to a *specific audience*. In this case, that *audience* is college students who are not politically active. The audience is *not* parents, congressional representatives, or bankers. Each of those audiences would need different rhetorical packages. What does *this* particular audience want and need? This question is intimately connected to the wording of your *message*. There are different ways to state every message, and a few word changes here and there can attract and/or repel different audiences. For example, the official message in the current example is "The government should bail out students rather than banks." But that could be changed to: "Banks got bailed out, students get sold out;" "Students before banks;" "Students vs. banks: you decide!" Each of these messages is more or less effective for different kinds of audiences. Regardless of the specifics, make sure that your message is as clear as possible. This means being clear in your own mind first. If you're confused about your own message, then others will be even more confused. What are you trying to say? What is the main point of your message? Will your audience be able to follow along and understand? Are you staying on point as you speak, write, act, converse, or facilitate?

One way to achieve such clarity is to consider the length of your message. This is not necessarily an issue during a teach-in, since you will be covering a swath of information in an educational setting. But length of message in other situations can be more important. Should it be one sentence, one paragraph, or one page? One minute, five minutes, or 20 minutes?

The general rule is to be concise and to the point—less is usually more. Also, think about how much space or time you need. You cannot cover the history of peace activism in a one-page statement or even an hour-long talk. Length of message is also an issue of *respect*. Audiences are giving you their time and attention. Taking up too much time might be interpreted as disrespectful. What do you want to say, and how much time will others grant you? It helps to refine your message—slim it down, make it more precise, and tweak it to the best of your ability: To do this, I suggest a four-step process:

1. Articulate your message into *one clear sentence*.
2. Explain your message (either to yourself or to others) in *one solid paragraph*.
3. Be prepared for *extended conversation*.
4. Turn your message into a *catchy sound bite*.

Sometimes you have time for only a single line. Other times you'll need something a little longer, and still others times you'll need a full explanation. Sound bites are almost always helpful, and you should create those *last*. This ensures that you truly understand your own message before you condense it into a couple of words. Condensing your message before you fully understand it may actually hinder your clarity.

All of this work should be done with the goal of *adapting your message to your audience*. This cannot be stressed enough. You might have a single idea (or similar ideas) that you use for multiple teach-ins, workshops, speeches, essays, pamphlets, and flyers. But always adapt and adjust that idea to each and every audience. High school students are different from college students; college students are different from recent graduates; and recent graduates are different from those who have never attended college. Rural Midwesterners are different from urban Northeasterners. African American females are different from Asian American males. The point is not to divide and differentiate people into reductive categories. Instead, it is to *understand* and *connect with* different people. As the famous labor organizer Saul Alinsky states:

> Communication with others takes place when they understand what you're trying to get across to them. If they don't understand, then you are not communicating regardless of words, pictures, or anything else. People only understand things in terms of their experience, which means that you must get within their experience. Further, communication is a two-way process. If you try to get your ideas across to others without paying attention to what they have to say to you, you can forget about the whole thing.[1]

We're all different, and sometimes we are *extremely* different from one another. But we can always find ways to connect with each other. As an activist, you need to find/create that connection and use it as a bridge. That bridge helps you move people to action.

Doing all of this is a lot of work. It takes time, thought, and patience. But we make the effort because we are trying to change the world. That's a lofty goal that often seems impossible. But it becomes easier and more achievable by improving your communication and rhetoric.

PART 2

WORKING WITH OTHERS

3

Participation and Democracy

JOSHUA RYAN HOLST

> *To glorify democracy and to silence the people is*
> *a farce; to discourse on humanism and to negate*
> *people is a lie.... For the truly humanist educator*
> *and the authentic revolutionary, the object of*
> *action is the reality to be transformed by*
> *them together with other people.*
>
> — PAULO FREIRE

WHETHER YOU CARE PASSIONATELY ABOUT THE ENVIRON-
ment, poverty, racism, war, the judicial system, or any other issue,
big or small, it is essential to understand the nature of democracy,
how we participate in it, and how we can actually create it. The purpose of this chapter is to help you learn to become *participants in*
and *creators of* democracy. In the following pages I will examine how
democracy works, breaking down the process from voting to lobbying. I will explore the role that social movements and demonstrations play in creating democracy outside the confines of the electoral
process. I will also explain how "direct democracy" and "deliberative
democracy" work, both within and outside of the state structure. In
this process, I will explore some of the challenges democracy faces
in its various forms, and how they can be overcome. Finally, I will

provide guidelines on how to actually practice democracy through deliberative, consensus decision-making procedures. But first it will be helpful to clarify what democracy is by looking at democratic practices throughout history.

Understanding Democracy: A Brief History

"Democracy" means a lot of things to different people. Democracy is on the lips of Western governments as they command their soldiers across the globe, but the same word has been used to mobilize insurgents fighting dictators that Western governments backed. In the US, neoliberal conservatives champion democracy in opposition to socialism, while anarchists protesting abuses of power champion democracy in opposition to neoliberalism. Even if you think you know what democracy is, its meaning can be confusing. For our purposes, "democracy" will be about the relationship between the public—the individuals and grassroots organizations that make up society—and the *decisions* that affect their lives.

Where does democracy come from? There are a lot of popular misunderstandings about democracy's origins. We should realize that democracy did *not* originate in the Western world and then spread to everywhere else. Democracies have actually been found throughout history all over the world. Perhaps the confusion is because the word "democracy" derives from Greek roots (*dêmos*, meaning *people*), or because Western elites sought to tie democracy to European antecedents in the course of creating a myth of the Western democratic state. The democracy of the Greek city-states was distinct from what we have today, however. In the 5th century BCE, when Pericles expanded Athenian citizenship from the *polis* to the *dêmos* (at that time, this meant expanding citizenship to the poorer classes), this gesture still accounted for only a small portion of the full population, considering that slaves and women were excluded. For those who qualified as citizens, Athenian democracy was far more participatory and direct than we see today: Athenian Assembly membership included any citizen who chose to attend, and some 500 officeholders were selected on a rotating basis by lot instead of election.[1]

The Greek city-states are a valuable historical example, but the truth is that classical political theory only came back to the West centuries after the Greek democracies had crumbled. This occurred by way of Middle Eastern scholars in the Muslim caliphates who had preserved, translated, and analyzed the Greek texts. Meanwhile, other democracies, independent of the Greek model, could be found around the world.

For much of the world's history, democracy survived in those communities that were able to escape the forced labor and political hierarchies of "civilizations": democracy could be found in places as varied as tribal governments, Buddhist monasteries, and pirate ships.[2] In Europe, the Vikings held democratic assemblies within a circle of stones called a *ting* until the aristocracies took hold and the role of *tings* changed.[3] According to anthropologist Pierre Clastres, Amazonian indigenous peoples were able to hold onto their relatively egalitarian way of life deep in the jungle by a combination of mobility and violent defense from first the Incan Empire and later the Spanish state. Some of those egalitarian groups in the Amazon were believed to be Incan communities that escaped the Incan Empire. Across the world in the remote highlands of Southeast Asia and the jungles of Indonesia, a wide range of village-level political organizations—from democratic to despotic—continue to exist; for much of the history of these indigenous communities, their cultural survival has relied upon evading the raids of empires that were searching for slave labor. Today, their continued existence rests upon their ability to elude the state form of government.[4]

DEMOCRACY is not a monolith. Different societies and communities approach "democracy" in different ways.

Democracy has flourished outside the nation-state system, but what of *inside* the nation-state system? Before we get to that, what is a state exactly? While the word "state" can be used to refer to specific US states under the federal government, it also has a separate meaning referring to a kind of political entity over a territory. Thus, the United States is also a state, while the Navajo Nation and nomad tribes in the Sahara would not be considered states. Today we often use the term "state" or "nation-state" to describe the countries we see on a political map. Some academics argue that this system developed in Europe as rural communities were violently incorporated under armed aristocratic control; local aristocrats were then consolidated into sovereign states after Cardinal Richelieu negotiated the Treaty of Westphalia in 1648.[5]

Democracy came to the nation-state system as a break with centuries of Western aristocracy, beginning with the American Revolution. A series of subsequent revolutions followed throughout Europe. As a federation of colonies competing for power, the revolutionary leaders of the United States needed to implement an alternative form of government in which power was shared. To do this, they drew on Western philosophers, but an indispensable influence may have been their contact with Native American peoples. A number of historians believe that the American Constitution and subsequent democratic institutions were influenced by contact with the Iroquois League. The Iroquois political system was a complex confederation, often involving democratic consensus decision-making, with specific powers separated among members of different nations and between men and women.[6] This implies that such celebrated and beloved concepts as liberty and equality did not spread from Western Europe to the rest of the world. There is evidence to suggest that contact with life outside the confines of the colonial state helped transmit these values to Euro-descended colonists as they interacted with Native American tribes in their daily lives.[7] This insight not only corrects historical misconceptions and challenges ethnocentrism, but it also helps to deepen our understanding of global democratic traditions. Democracy has been occurring for a very long time and has been practiced by a multitude of populations.

This segues into my next point: democracy is not an absolute that rests neatly between lines on a map—e.g., *this* country has a democracy and *that* country does not. Instead, it's more like a cluster of muddled grey areas that vary over time and space. This is because the heart of democracy is based on decisions. Within democracies, various decisions are made with democratic involvement (such as who is the best performer on *American Idol*), while other decisions are negotiated by international elites (such as whether environmental laws banning cancer-causing substances violate trade agreements). Consequently, democracy applies only to certain spaces and certain issues, never to a country as a whole.

In all political systems, some decisions are made democratically and others are not. Many, and even most, decisions within the United States are decided through *non-democratic* procedures. On the other hand, democratic enclaves can also claim space in otherwise authoritarian environments: for example, anarchist-controlled neighborhoods in Barcelona rebelling under the Spanish dictator Franco, Guangxi's village governments in Mao's China, or the public defender's office under Peruvian dictator Fujimori.[8] In this vein, activists frustrated with representative democracy have created spaces of consensus community decision-making in sites of protest. Some anarchist theorists refer to these various spaces of democracy as "Temporary Autonomous Zones" (TAZs).[9] Autonomist squatters in Italy use the TAZ strategy to create democratic pockets in abandoned buildings, while a coalition of indigenous peoples and environmental activists in the Minnehaha Free State of Minnesota created a TAZ to block the demolition of an indigenous burial ground. However, some autonomous zones are far from temporary. In Chiapas, Mexico, large portions of the Lacandon Jungle are ruled by an Indigenous Congress drawing on indigenous political configurations that predate the Mexican government. Similarly, the indigenous movement in Ecuador is a complex composite of varied democratic traditions from its diverse nationalities.

Again, the main point here is this: *public involvement in making decisions is what makes a democracy democratic.* From the Western democracies of the nation-state to the Amazonian indigenous governments, different decisions involve the public in different ways—and many decisions don't involve the public at all. Keeping an eye on *which* decisions are democratic and the particular *way* the public is involved is critical for analyzing democracy. As a result, some activists argue that Western democracy isn't particularly democratic at all.

The Workings of Western Democracy

According to a 2006 poll, over a third of US citizens felt that voting in *American Idol*, a reality TV singing contest, mattered more than voting for the president of the country.[10] Whether you fall into that third or not, it's important to understand exactly what voting has to do with democracy. In American political elections, many people feel like they are presented with two bad choices. Commentators often blame this on the negative advertising that is used in campaigns. This may be the case, but there seems to be more at work than just negative advertising. It can be genuinely difficult to figure out what candidates actually stand for, particularly when they deceive the public and/or stretch the truth in debates and speeches. Meanwhile, the mainstream mass media almost never investigates actual voting records of the candidates, which would provide an understanding of what could be expected if they are elected. The media instead tends to focus on scandals and hollow rhetoric. At state and local levels, voters are often unfamiliar with the names of the candidates until they walk into the voting booth, and even fewer voters know the actual policies and how those policies will affect their lives.

Among younger US citizens, voter turnout tends to hover around 50 percent for presidential elections and 25 percent for midterm elections, while local officials have been successfully elected by less than four percent of their districts.[11] Meanwhile, the number of citizens legally barred from voting has steadily risen since 1971: for example, in California, approximately 20 percent of the voting age population is barred from voting.[12] Poverty is another hindrance to voting: in 2000, only 35 percent of US voters in the poorest fifth turned out, while more than 71 percent of the wealthiest quintile voted.[13] A disproportionate percentage of the electorate thus favors politicians who, most likely, will benefit the wealthy rather than the poor.

The wealthy also disproportionately hold positions of government power. A famous study by sociologist Ralph Miliband showed that the wealthiest 0.5 percent of Americans occupy strategic positions within the judiciary and executive branches of the government and its attendant agencies.[14] Another sociologist, C. Wright Mills, argued that the control of the "power elite" over the government leaves ordinary citizens powerless.[15] Whose wants and needs are really represented by our government and politicians? Such issues help us understand why some people believe that voting for *American Idol* is more relevant than voting for the president. Perhaps viewers feel *American Idol* is more democratic than our political system.

That said, people often forget that voting is only one step in participating in democracy; once your candidate is elected, your work has just begun. The heads of multinational corporations don't cast their vote for a candidate and then simply walk away. After corporations organize collective funds to finance candidate campaigns, corporate lobbyists and corporate-funded think tanks spend the next four years making sure that politicians follow through on their promised agendas—agendas that most likely benefit profits at the expense of social programs, environmental protections, and small-business entrepreneurship. *Who* is in office is relevant only if it affects what they *do* while they are in office.

When elected officials are deciding to place a toxic waste dump in a particular neighborhood or to pass a law that lowers the standards for cancerous substances in the water supply, they are thinking about their reelection. Reelection requires a combination of votes and money. Portions of the electorate are organized into blocs; democratic clubs, organized labor, and community organizations, for instance, will follow particular politicians and will make endorsements to deliver votes. Endorsements from student associations, environmentalists, or unions can be used by candidates to draw large communities of voters who support a given cause. Unfortunately, more and more of the American electorate is socially atomized, meaning they aren't connected to community organizations, and they get their political information from going home and watching television after work. When people rely on the media instead of community organizations for their political information, *money*—largely spent on pamphlets, media campaigns, and campaign consultants—becomes more important for reelection.

If poor Latinos make up 18 percent of an elected official's district, and only 25 percent of them actually vote, they become an expendable demographic. The elected official must weigh the lost votes against the campaign money s/he will be able to get for placing that toxic waste dump in the Latino neighborhood. On the other hand, if activists in that Latino neighborhood form a voting bloc and engage the elected official, as well as allies outside of the community, through demonstrations, media exposure, and advocacy, then they may be able to stop that toxic dump from coming to their neighborhood. In other words, they must threaten the elected official's chances for reelection.

In order to prevent the uncertainties of reelection, elected officials sometimes "gerrymander" their voting districts. Gerrymandering occurs when the boundaries of a voting district are reconfigured to favor one party or voting bloc over another. A district might tend to vote 51% Republican and 49% Democrat, for instance. Before the next election, the Democrats might find a way to either expand or shrink their voting district to give them the upper hand—the new district now has more Democrats than Republicans, helping them win the election. In gerrymandered districts, election primaries are particularly important because they determine the *primary candidates* of each party. Five Democrats and five Republicans might run for office, but only one candidate from each party will make the final ticket—those final candidates are elected in the primaries. Since far fewer people vote in the primaries, it is fairly easy to gerrymander a particular district in order to steal a few extra votes.

Competitive elections are not necessarily a hallmark of a well-functioning democracy. This is due, in part, to the fact that competitive elections are expensive. In more competitive elections, both sides must raise more money and, consequently, owe favors to the wealthy interests that supported them. Corporations commonly support both sides, in the hope that their interests will be pursued regardless of the winner. In other cases, networks of competing corporations support opposing sides. Citizen interests become subordinated to the interests of money and nepotism, and elections become driven by empty rhetoric.

Money is an indispensable component of Western politics; no matter how much you may like a candidate, s/he must raise a minimum amount of money to stand a chance in an election. Still, in places where the electorate is socially thick—meaning full of active community organizations—candidates who are greatly outspent may still win if they have the support of the community.

The relationships between voters, money, social atomization, campaigns, and candidate positions can get complicated. Let me explain how this all works with an example: California Assembly member Betsy Butler authored a bill that required companies to provide shade for farmworkers, angering agribusiness corporations. Farmworkers have a machine pushing them through a giant field picking vegetables as fast as they can for approximately two dollars an hour. They spend all day in the sun, often getting sick from dehydration and pesticide exposure. Heat-related deaths have occurred, but since many farmworkers are not citizens, they have limited recourse to pressure politicians. The governor vetoed Butler's bill, but agribusiness companies wanted her out of office before she tried something else. These corporations founded a political action committee called Family Farmers for a Better California, and spent 250,000 dollars on mailers claiming that Butler supported child molesters. The mailers were complete with pictures of sad children looking recently molested. During Butler's reelection campaign, voters who were connected to networks of democratic clubs, farmworker unions, and civil rights organizations supported her. But those voters who were socially atomized relied on mailers and other corporate-funded advertisements. As might be expected, these voters believed that Butler supported child molesters, and consequently she lost the election. The lesson here is twofold. First, well-meaning elected officials are constantly fighting an uphill battle that is infused with corporate money, and therefore they must make careful political calculations if they want to stay in office. And second, voters do themselves a disservice by not organizing and participating in some type of collective effort.

Unfortunately, as more people become disenchanted with politics, the less they vote. Globally, voter turnout has been steadily declining for the last 50 years. However, other forms of political participation—donating to campaigns, conducting advocacy events, participating in boycotts and demonstrations—have been on the rise all over the world.[16] The critical issue thus becomes *how* we participate in democracy, which is the topic of the next section.

The Democracy of Demonstrations

Analysts have observed that the economic interests of the poor are rarely addressed by the government when citizens constrain themselves to working only within the system. According to social movement scholars Frances Fox Piven and Richard A. Cloward, "It is usually when unrest among the lower class breaks out of the confines of electoral procedures that the poor may have some influence, for the instability and polarization they then threaten to create by their actions in the factories or in the streets may force some response from electoral leaders."[17] In fact, rioting was the primary way for elites to know the will of the general public in much of Western history from Imperial Rome to 18th-century England.[18] Luckily, burning and pillaging isn't the only option; the United States has a rich tradition of nonviolent protests, everything ranging from a group of families refusing to allow their homes to be demolished to the mobilizations of millions for Occupy Wall Street. Successful social movements often use multiple strategies at once: for example, a social movement might organize a series of demonstrations, but it will also conduct local teach-ins and workshops, write op-eds for the newspaper, distribute flyers and pamphlets, build broad coalitions, and lobby local and state officials. In other words, social change often relies upon a multi-pronged approach that involves, but is not limited to, street demonstrations.

Social movements themselves come in all forms, from militantly hierarchical to highly democratic. However, some of the most sig-

nificant mobilizations in recent US history came from social movements following anarchist-influenced democratic principles. While
most people involved in these groups were neither anarchists nor
aware of the connection between their movement and anarchism,
the central organizers relied on anarchist approaches to democracy
in building the movements. For these organizers, the movement itself is an opportunity to challenge hierarchy and to create a space
where people can act democratically for the common good.

It's not just the movement's agenda that matters—
the democracy that the movement creates in the
process of mobilizing is also (and perhaps even
more) important.

The anti-globalization movement makes an
excellent case study of democracy in action. The
movement's best-known protest occurred at the
1999 meeting of the World Trade Organization
(WTO) in Seattle, Washington. Civil society organizations[19] throughout the world had watched small
businesses, subsistence farmers, labor rights, access to jobs, public
health, and environmental regulations suffer as the WTO dissolved
local laws in favor of international businesses. Unions, school teachers, university students, environmentalists, human rights activists,
and individual citizens of all sorts descended on downtown Seattle
in enormous numbers to shut down the WTO. This provoked a series of subsequent mobilizations against the WTO, as well as against
the World Bank, the International Monetary Fund, free trade agreements, and other meetings of international elites, all over the world.

The media often portray such demonstrations as being utterly
chaotic, but that is not true. These demonstrations are actually rich
exercises in human cooperation. As things turn tense between the
police and the protesters at a demonstration, some groups work together to block police cars, while others help secure escape routes for
international guest speakers who might get deported. One person
might shout a command and rationale: "Make a path for people who
can't go to jail and need to leave. Repeat!" Waves of people then shout

the same sentence further down, making a path as they shout. This is human coordination in action.

One broad coalition central to the Seattle WTO protest, the Direct Action Network (DAN), was committed to nonhierarchical anarchist principles and engaged existing social movements throughout the United States. Each group's education campaign increased awareness, and increased the numbers of those wanting to mobilize. Meanwhile, new Internet news outlets, such as Indymedia, reported not only on the environmental and human rights issues surrounding the expansion of global business, but on the protest movements against those abuses. For example, protesters reading online about companies who left the United States in order to open in places where environmental laws were weak and labor leaders were assassinated could also read where to protest the international organizations facilitating that process.

The Seattle protest itself was a very complex and highly democratic endeavor involving everyone from lawyers and homeless people to feminists and longshoremen. Coordinated at multiple levels, the core of the protest involved affinity groups: groups of about six to 12 people who made consensus decisions on where to go and what to do. At times, multiple affinity groups would combine for a joint activity, such as locking each other's arms to block WTO officials from entering the building, or engaging in education activities with the surrounding community. DAN coordinated medical camps with trained volunteers, communications teams, and teams of lawyers prepared to defend jailed protesters. Many protesters remarked on the sense of community they felt as a result of participating, and that particular experience, as much as shutting down the WTO itself, was the point. DAN acted as a nonhierarchical facilitator that engaged volunteers to share their expertise and join in making decisions. In that sense, then, DAN produced a democracy.

This push didn't begin in the United States. The inspiration for DAN and other activist groups to commence this wave of activity was a call to action against the WTO at an *encuentro* in Mexico in 1996 organized by the Zapatista rebels. This was the rebels' first *encuen-*

tro, that is, a meeting of social movements from all over the world committed to egalitarianism. The Zapatista rebellion itself began in southern Mexico. Although they had been organizing for years underground, the Zapatistas announced themselves to the world on January 1, 1994—the same day that the North American Free Trade Agreement (NAFTA) (an economic contract between Canada, the United States, and Mexico) was signed into effect. Prior to the start of their rebellion (kicked off by kidnapping the governor of Chiapas), the Zapatistas had mobilized *consultas* throughout Mexico, urging civil society groups—the elderly, women, disabled, ethnic groups, any organization that was interested—to meet and discuss relevant questions: "How do you feel about NAFTA?" "Do you feel your government represents your interests?" "What do we need to do to protect our rights?" When the Zapatista rebellion began, civil society mobilized in support and demonstrated in Mexico City, thus making a military-led massacre politically unfeasible. Within Chiapas, the Zapatistas blockaded roads built for timber companies invading indigenous territory. They helped defend autonomous zones ruled by indigenous governments. Unlike most rebellions, their goal—within not only Chiapas, but all of Mexico—was *not* for themselves take control of the state, but to encourage *the expansion of democracy*.

Dilemmas of Democracy

What should this expansion of democracy look like? At the WTO protest in Seattle, it was common to hear protesters express chants calling for "direct democracy." The idea was that WTO decisions—which affect everything from jobs to labor rights, human health, and the environment—should directly involve the public. Direct democracy, as opposed to representative democracy, takes power out of the hands of elected officials and places it into the hands of the public. Proponents imagine that, if only the public had the opportunity, they would counteract the actions of corrupt elected officials that place public health and human rights at risk. When protesters make calls for direct democracy, they mean that they want popular control over these kinds of decisions. But the term "direct democracy" can be misleading. In organizing the protest, anarchist-influenced DAN organizers utilized a model that was more than just direct democracy: it involved consensus decision-making. I will say more about consensus decision-making later on, but first I want to look more closely at direct democracy in its simplest form.

In some cases, direct democracy is actually implemented by the state; this might include, for instance, national referendums, popular recalls of elected officials, and ballot propositions. The results of these practices are mixed. Sometimes direct democracy produces the popular control over the state that activists dream of, but that's not always the case. Simply putting issues to a vote doesn't always produce the direct democracy activists are imagining. While there are cases where direct democracy has worked well, I'm going to outline some examples in which direct democracy was not as successful as we would hope.

Ballot propositions are a particularly important example of direct democracy. They allow the electorate to vote directly on policies that affect them, and can produce exciting results. However, propositions are often the most effective tool of private interests. Before election time, you see countless ads spinning narratives for why you should vote for or against a proposition. These ads are often fantasies that have very little to do with the actual proposition itself. For example, in 2004, Californians watched ads for Proposition 64. In one ad, an average-looking car mechanic gets out from underneath a car and talks about how unfair lawsuits will destroy his business and how small business owners like him need voters to vote "yes" on Proposition 64—the purpose of which was to protect people like him from greedy lawyers. But in reality, the ad campaign was funded by a consortium of multinational oil companies and grocery chains rather than small businesses. The proposition passed, nullifying the law that previously had allowed lawyers to sue (1) produce companies that had sold bottled water that contained arsenic; and (2) oil companies that had illegally exposed a neighborhood to cancer-causing waste for decades. Voters who read the tiny blurb about unfair lawsuits in their voting booklet probably didn't realize that they had voted away their right to defend themselves against companies that place them at risk for cancer.

In the Proposition 64 case, people believed that this actor represented small businesses when in fact he was paid by a coalition of corporations. With the help of public relations firms, corporations can create their own community organizations or even sponsor surrogate organizations in order to mask their influence. Rather than a *grassroots* movement, you have an *astroturf* movement.

ASTROTURF "movements" are used by **INSTITUTIONS OF POWER** to generate a bandwagon effect. People are **TRICKED** into believing that a majority of the public **SUPPORTS** a cause, and people then jump on the **BANDWAGON.**

When thinking about democracy, direct or otherwise, it is important to remember that governments, parties, and multinational corporations can and do use the same strategies as social movements. They hire community organizers to conduct petitions and demonstrations, and they mobilize polished media campaigns. In Los Angeles, waste management companies mobilized people to call and write their elected officials to request a landfill in their neighborhood. Using a combination of public relations and activist techniques, the companies were able to convince people to place a dump in their own neighborhood.

Public intellectual Noam Chomsky explains why this type of phenomenon shouldn't be surprising:

> When you can't control people by force, and when the voice of the people can be heard you have this problem...and therefore you have to control what people think. And the standard way to do this is to resort to what in more honest days used to be called propaganda, manufacture of consent, creation of necessary illusion.[20]

This has been going on in the US for some time, with increasing sophistication. The famous war propagandist Edward Bernays, nephew of Sigmund Freud, founded the discipline of public relations, using his uncle's theories to manipulate the general public. For Bernays, propaganda was necessary to keep the unruliness of democracy at bay. In his book *Propaganda*, Bernays writes that "those who manipulate this unseen mechanism of society constitute an invisible government which is the true ruling power of our country" and that "the conscious and intelligent manipulation of the organized habits and opinions of the masses is an important element in democratic society."[21] Hired by tobacco companies to make smoking acceptable for women, Bernays was responsible for feminists lighting "freedom torches" as a political statement.

Manipulation of the public is not the only problem with democracy: discrimination and prejudice can also run rampant in democracies. This second problem with democracy, direct or otherwise, is what Alexis de Tocqueville termed "the tyranny of the majority." During the public debates on gay marriage, a flurry of propositions were passed across various states in the US in order to ban gay marriage, a move which served no purpose other than discrimination. The expansion of democracy can also mean the expansion of xenophobia and religious repression. The new democracies of the Arab Spring have brought with them a rise in church burning and violence against religious minorities. This is a problem shared by many religions: India's transition to democracy brought the Hindu-Muslim violence of the Partition, and Indian Catholics were forced into religious reeducation camps.[22] This goes back to the very beginnings of democracy. The first Bill of Rights in England—predecessor to the highly valued Bills of Rights in France and the US—had sections dedicated to barring Catholics from participation in England's Protestant government.

My point with the above examples is that democracy, even direct democracy, has vulnerabilities. The expansion of democracy can be used as a tool for discriminatory majorities or wealthy business interests to violate the rights of minorities. When the general population is consulted on an issue without the opportunity to deliberate and without the correct information, direct democracy devolves into a public relations battle determined more by money than by the protection of rights. Democratic space can be a tool for the majority to discriminate against minorities based upon religion, ethnicity, sex, or sexual orientation.

Deliberative Democracy

To avoid the tyranny of the majority, many activists stress that consensus and its arduous deliberation are integral to democracy. The activist vision of direct democracy is therefore incomplete without consensus. Anthropologist David Graeber explains why egalitarian societies outside the state structure usually involve assemblies that strive for deliberation and consensus instead of voting: "If there is no way to compel those who find a majority decision distasteful to go along with it, then the last thing one would want to do is to hold a vote.... Voting would be the most likely means to guarantee the sort of humiliations, resentments, and hatreds that ultimately lead to the destruction of communities."[23] In other words, there is a difference between a direct democracy that is predicated on voting, and a *deliberative* direct democracy that is built on consensus decision-making.

Deliberative democracy involves the art of public deliberation, i.e., public discussion and debate of ideas and issues. This term is an umbrella that covers a wide range of democratic forms, but the strongest are those that engage individuals at more intimate, grassroots levels. When deliberation and direct democracy are combined, it can make democracy more participatory, decisions better, and rights stronger. Paolo Freire, an education activist and philosopher in Brazil, saw great possibilities for liberation in dialogue. He argued that democracy was best served not by political leaders pushing agendas (no matter how well-meaning), but by a program of sharing knowledge and experiences to work together to combat oppression.[24] Freire's organizing strategies were so effective that Brazil's military government imprisoned, then exiled, him in the 1960s.

A critical place to experiment with deliberative direct democracy is within our own social organizations. If we make democracy ourselves, it will spread. The recent Occupy Wall Street (OWS) movement was driven by participatory, deliberative democratic practices.

The OWS movement began in September 2011. It was motivated in part by the Arab Spring, which was an uprising that started in Tunisia in December 2010. That action in Tunisia led to another uprising in Egypt during the spring of 2011. What followed were a series of uprisings throughout North African and Middle Eastern countries.

WE ARE THE 99 PERCENT!

American activists were energized by these (and other) actions and felt compelled to challenge the economic inequality and political corruption that occurs in the US.

Operation Empire State Rebellion (OESR) was an early test run for the Occupy movement. OESR called for people to occupy Zuccotti Park, which is located next to Wall Street in Lower Manhattan, in June 2011. Only four people showed up. But another organization found inspiration in this effort and held a "People's General Assembly" two months later. David Graeber, whom I quoted above, was one of the people attending. The assembly wasn't particularly democratic, so Graeber and a dozen anarchist-minded friends promptly held another assembly in a corner of the park. They discussed their own issues and demands, and soon all of the attendees decided to join in the more democratic discussion on how to occupy Wall Street. They broke up into working groups and labored for weeks to achieve a working consensus. These efforts were aided by the call put out by *Ad Busters*, an anti-consumer magazine, to occupy Wall Street on September 17. A thousand people arrived the first day, but were prevented from staying by police. That did not stop the protestors. In early October, hundreds of people were arrested while marching over the Brooklyn Bridge. With increasing media coverage, a spark was lit. Hundreds of occupations soon popped up all over the US and across the world. Within months, a group of four had given birth to a movement of millions.[25] From Johannesburg, South Africa, to Casper, Wyoming, people occupied spaces in front of businesses and city halls. These occupations held assemblies where participants engaged in consensus decision-making and direct democracy. Various issues were brought to the attention of international media. The political discussion in the United States suddenly focused on the divide between the "one percent" and the "99 percent."

The OWS movement started with just four people and soon swept the whole world. Democracy is something you can make, even with just a few people working together. If we cultivate it, if we improve it, it can grow. The next section explores what this might look like in practice.

Making Democracy

Democracy begins with you. Now that you know more about it, how do you make the world an increasingly democratic place? How do you engage in consensus decision-making and practice facilitation? How do you promote equality among your peers? How do you spread democracy on your own?

Consensus Decision-Making

As with the anti-globalization movement, consensus decision-making was a central part of the Occupy movement's vast popularity. At the movement level, when platforms are developed in collaboration with diverse groups, they appeal to a wider group of people. At the individual level, when people feel that they are a part of the decision-making process, they devote more energy to the task at hand.

Conducting a democratic meeting sounds simple, but that is not always the case. Before you even begin discussing the tasks at hand, there may be extensive debates over such issues as "How do we want to discuss issues?" or "Should we take turns speaking clockwise or counterclockwise?" As one might imagine, such conversations can be tedious, tense, and tiresome. This demonstrates that consensus does not always work well in all situations for all decisions. When the Zapatistas organize their *consultas* or Occupy activists organize their General Assemblies, they already have an idea of what topics they are and are not going to discuss. Careful thought should be given to which topics should be dealt with using consensus, which topics can be handled beforehand behind the scenes, and which topics can be delegated to individuals or constituent groups.

Consensus decision-making is particularly valuable when hammering out a shared platform, figuring out who has what expertise, or seeking to recruit involvement in a collective activity. In recruiting coalitions, it's important to keep in mind that different organizations (such as unions, farmer associations, nonprofit organizations, and student groups) all have their own histories, philosophies, and internal power dynamics. They are rarely internally egalitarian, and people from hierarchical organizations will inevitably carry those hierarchies with them to coalition decision-making bodies, even if they are consensus-based. But recruiting people from the right positions within constituent organizations to engage in consensus decision-making can be critical for spanning boundaries between organizations and acting collaboratively for a common cause.

Still, consensus should be handled with care. Anthropologist Laura Nader suggests that the desire for harmony may propagate inequality[26]—we often sacrifice important minority rights and interests because we are taught to value getting along. Proponents of radical democracy, as conceived by Ernesto Laclau and Chantal Mouffe, make a similar argument: that pluralistic difference should be celebrated instead of consensus.[27] For them, the push for consensus in consensus decision-making can ultimately be a form of domination. While consensus is a valuable goal, it should never be imperative, as we will discuss further in the section "Break Into Smaller Groups."

Even with the best of intentions, maintaining a participatory, egalitarian group is difficult work. That raises the second point, which is facilitation.

Learn Facilitation Techniques
Instead of Leadership Techniques

Democracy is about placing leadership in the hands of the people. That's why the Occupy movement and other groups with an anarchist influence often resist choosing leaders, at least in the traditional sense. Instead of making executive decisions like hierarchical leaders, a facilitator leads the process of decision-making. The facilitator's role is to guide a group's discussion, but *not* to exercise hierarchical control over the outcome. It's harder than it sounds. It takes a great deal of skill and practice to facilitate, but life is full of opportunities to practice, whether you are organizing your fellow workers to start a new union, doing a group project for school, or deciding what kind of pizza to order with some friends.

There are plenty of books on the topic, but learning by participating in a group that uses facilitation is invaluable. Keep in mind that there are many different kinds of facilitation. Some are very structured: "Only speak when holding the stick, please. Your one minute and 45 seconds of speaking time is finished." Other forms can be more organic, focused on guiding and consciously monitoring group dynamics. Some student and community groups develop unique techniques for consensus as they practice collaborating with each other and teaching new people who join the group. Other facilitation techniques have been developed formally.

Different facilitators have different goals: facilitators negotiating political agreements or social workers interacting with youth will have different agendas from a facilitator seeking to promote democracy. The focus of facilitating a democratic meeting should be not consensus but participation. It is not uncommon for one person to verbally dominate the group decision-making process. Meanwhile, another person might provide a type of secondary support that allows his or her friend to occupy a dominant position in the group. Still another person might be disengaged and not put in any effort or work. Another type of person, typically very quiet, does a lot of the work but is secretly angry with the unfair way the group is functioning. A facilitator should try to be aware of these dynamics and establish a pathway for more egalitarian discussion and participation among *all* group members.

Facilitating democracy does not have to follow a rigid system of order; it can be an organic, interaction that taps deeply into the collective desires and resources of everyone involved. There are many approaches that draw from, for example, process-oriented psychology, systems theory, and/or communication theory. There are a multitude of books on facilitation, both practical and theoretical. One book worth looking into is *Small Group Decision Making: Communication and the Group Process*, by Donald G. Ellis and B. Aubrey Fisher. It's not a formula for facilitation, but it can sensitize the reader to the underlying dynamics at work in small groups using a systems theory lens. That knowledge can help you gently guide the process in order to enhance participation in decision-making.

If done correctly, consensus decision-making is an excellent way to negotiate the tensions between expertise and equality, so that each individual can tap into their unique reserves of knowledge and the group can reach its full potential. Many facilitators employ a Freirian method to pool expertise. Through his books *Pedagogy of the Oppressed* and *Education for Critical Consciousness*, Paolo Freire, the Brazilian intellectual mentioned previously, has had a profound influence on those seeking to address inequality. Freire's egalitarian model of education is about pooling the valuable and diverse knowledge and skills from lived experience that all people have, to move toward the common goal of equality. Instead of imposing ideas, Freirian educators abandon authority and hierarchy in order to learn from and collaborate with their peers through dialogue and deliberation. As a component of democratic action, facilitated deliberation is a way to break our own internalized oppression. If successful, it can help us escape the machinations of elites like Bernays or PR firms that mobilize us against our own interests. In consensus decision-making, a Freirian approach is a way to take stock of the unique knowledge and skills participants bring to the discussion, and fully utilize them.

Break into Smaller Groups

Ultimately, full participation requires breaking from a larger group into smaller groups. It's virtually impossible for a thousand people to have in-depth deliberation, but six people certainly can. Upon rejoining the full group, the conclusions of the smaller groups can be integrated more easily. Other reasons for breaking into groups are to assign tasks or utilize expertise—be it a dance committee at a school or an appropriations committee in the US Congress. That's key for both the division of labor and utilizing expertise in a large organization.

One more reason to break into groups is that, while consensus can be achieved on some issues, in other cases consensus may be impossible or even undesirable. As mentioned previously, consensus can be used as a bludgeon to dominate dissenters. To avoid this, when sub-groups of people strongly disagree on an issue, they should be free to maintain their autonomy on that issue. That doesn't mean the group as a whole has to dissolve; it just means you collaborate where you can, and you don't where you can't.

Expand your Network to Share Information and Build Solidarity

Facilitating egalitarian, democratic deliberation as described above is essential. But even with deliberation, misinformation and manipulation may continue to plague democratic decision-making. Key to combatting this problem are networking, solidarity, and information sharing.

Deep in the Amazon rainforest, I met a woman whose husband had died, and all but one of her children had become severely ill. This was likely related to the contaminants in her water supply from a gold mine that was operating upstream. The only doctor available worked for the mining company, and he neglected to tell her why her children were sick and her husband was dead. When she told me her story, she started crying; she believed her misfortune was because God hated her.

Mining companies are often required to secure consent from local towns in order to mine. In some cases, Amazonian villages may then engage in a very egalitarian, democratic process before deciding to allow the mining companies to operate in exchange for some chickens and bags of rice. Ten years later, food is scarce, and pollution-related illnesses are rampant. Without access to the right information from the beginning, indigenous peoples are easily manipulated by community relations experts.

Information is a critical and often elusive piece of the democratic puzzle. This chapter has touched on multiple examples where information and misinformation have been used to subvert democracy: a doctor working for a mining company convincing indigenous peoples that there is no pollution; a public relations firm in Los Angeles mobilizing residents to request a landfill that will poison their water; Edward Bernays convincing feminists that smoking "freedom torches" is the route to liberation.

Networking with organizations (such as doctors concerned with smoking or environmental organizations concerned with toxics from landfills) is critical to ensure that democratic decision-making is informed. Building bridges with communities that have faced similar situations is essential. In the case of the indigenous peoples in the Ecuadorian Amazon, the environmental nonprofit Acción Ecológica works with indigenous groups that are contacted by mining companies. Not only do they connect them to doctors and lawyers, but they bring them to see other indigenous communities where mining has happened, enabling villagers to see firsthand the impacts of mining—an opportunity for indigenous communities to not only learn from each other's experiences, but to also become bonded in solidarity and political will.

Conclusion

Whether democracy comes in the form of America's founding Constitution, an Amazonian Shuar tribe joining the indigenous movement, or anarchist squatters forming a TAZ, making democracy is about inventing new traditions that build upon the past to address the present.

The democratic processes described in this chapter are all imperfect, because democracy is always a work in progress. Democracy isn't synonymous with elections, public office, or any static political structures. Democracy isn't something that's handed to us from the government at all; we *make* democracy when we take popular, deliberative, democratic control over the decisions that affect our lives. Even exemplary movements like the OWS didn't fully deal with our social inequalities. The democratic improvements they introduced did not eliminate all of democracy's vulnerabilities, but they are great steps in the right direction and great opportunities to improve democratic practice.

Democracy is a struggle that is never finished. In fact, everything that you learn in this book, from interpersonal skills to communication strategies to conference planning to social media, can bring us closer to democratic practice. Now that you know the nature of democracy and some of its potential pitfalls, you are in a better position to create a more democratic world. In the process, you can address the issues that are most important to you and your communities.

Transformative Justice and Conflict Transformation[1]

ANTHONY J. NOCELLA II, MELISSA CHIPRIN,
ANNIESSA ANTAR, AND ALISHA PAGE
(MEMBERS OF SAVE THE KIDS)

> *It is absolutely essential that the oppressed participate*
> *in the revolutionary process with an increasingly critical*
> *awareness of their role as subjects of the transformation.*
> — PAULO FREIRE

THIS CHAPTER IS DEDICATED TO INTRODUCING ALTERNATIVE processes of punitive justice and addressing conflict. This chapter first introduces and defines conflict and discusses why it is important for activists to understand it. Then, after explaining different ways to approach and manage conflict, the chapter introduces conflict transformation — a holistic, educational, empowering, and accountability-inducing process. Finally, this chapter compares and contrasts restorative justice and transformative justice.

Attaining Peace: Guns, Guards, and Prisons?

Conflict and injustices surround us on a daily basis. It is surprising and disappointing, then, that we are not taught in schools, from kindergarten to the 12th grade and beyond, how to manage, resolve,

83

and/or transform conflict. The answer of the National Rifle Association (NRA) to the 2012 shooting at Sandy Hook Elementary School in Newtown, Connecticut, where the 20-year-old shooter, Adam Lanza, killed 26 people, including 20 children, is to have armed guards placed in every school around the country. So, in the eyes of the NRA, gun violence should be countered with *more guns*. In many economically disadvantaged urban communities of color in the US, this answer is already a reality, in addition to cameras at every corner of the school building and metal detectors at every entrance of the school. So far, this solution doesn't seem to be working.

Famed public intellectual Cornel West recognizes this reality and wonders why there is so much outrage and sorrow when white children are shot, but so little outrage and sorrow when youth of color are shot, which occurs much more regularly. In the wake of the Newtown shooting, West states, "Not a mumbling word when the black folk getting shot. But now Newtown, CT, vanilla side, low and behold.... We have a major conversation. That's wonderful. Each life is precious, but it just upsets me when we're so differential."[2] Here, West is addressing issues of identity and privilege. In general, people in dominant positions of power (e.g., presidents, the media, entertainers and celebrities) tend to cater to dominant identities, such as those who are white, Christian, able-bodied, male, heterosexual, formally educated, and wealthy. Conversely, people of color, people who identify as LGBTQ, females, those who are economically disadvantaged and/or not formally educated, and folks with disabilities are commonly silenced, marginalized, and/or ignored. These folks do not receive the same kind of attention and care, even when they are victims of direct violence. This is an injustice, to say the least, and very telling about our society.

Some people believe that more prisons are the answer—that we can attain a more peaceful and just society by "getting more criminals off the street." But who is a criminal? It's a known fact that someone caught with cocaine, which is a high-end drug, does less prison time than someone caught with crack cocaine, which is a low-end drug. And what should be the focus of the criminal justice system—

to punish offenders or to help offenders transform themselves into better people?

As members of Save the Kids, an organization grounded in transformative justice, prison abolition, and Hip Hop activism, we are very familiar with these debates since much of our own community organizing, activism, and scholarship is focused on the problems of the current criminal justice system. Our work is influenced by former and current prisoners, oppressed communities, and critical criminology scholarship. In general, critical criminology opposes punitive retribution and exploitive "justice" systems, which are cornerstones of the US prison system. In the early 1980s, there were approximately 500,000 adults housed in the US prison system. But by the end of the decade, there were more than a million people incarcerated.[3] In the 1990s, education was taken out of the prisons in order to save money, and it was replaced with factory jobs that profited corporations.[4] In many ways, this substitution of jobs for education is a form of incarcerated slavery that funds the prison industrial complex. The criminal justice system eventually became so overcrowded and unmanageable that there were not enough lawyers, judges, and courtrooms to properly handle all the cases. The prison industrial complex soon influenced the criminal justice system to become more of an industry dishing out punishments than a place for justice for the community and victims. Then, in the early 2000s, under President George W. Bush, the US prison population grew to more than two million, which actually overextended the prison bed limit.[5] With no more room in prisons, the government now commonly imprisons people in their own homes with ankle bracelets and other surveillance devices. This whole operation has developed along a logic of privatization: more and more prisons and prison services are becoming privately owned. Certain people and corporations now have a monetary incentive to incarcerate people, which influences state and federal laws and policies within the criminal justice system.

Sex-trafficked prostitution is but one example of this relationship between incarceration and profit. Most people think of prostitution as a choice. In some cases that may be true, and in that case one might argue that prostitution should be legalized. But very few people understand the relationship between sex trafficking and forced prostitution. According to the website ProCon.org, under its entry for "prostitution" (2014), California made 11,334 arrests, Texas made 7,555 arrests, and Florida made 5,048 arrests for illegal prostitution in the year 2010.[6] As can be seen, illegal prostitution provides a guaranteed prison population and, thus, a guaranteed profit. But how many of these arrestees actually chose, on their own accord, to engage in prostitution? How many were instead forced into it via sex trafficking? We agree with members of Sex Trafficking Survivors United that the victims and survivors of sex-trafficked prostitution need to be highlighted in public discourse.[7] The discussion too often involves the silencing and blaming of victims. A more transformative approach would allow victims and survivors to tell their stories, which means that we, the general public, would listen, understand, and empathize. It would also involve addressing the male demand of humans for sex, which primarily involves young girls and women, but also young gay men and transgender people. This multipronged approach addresses numerous issues, people, and structures in order to uproot the problem and transform the surrounding conditions.[8]

Wisdom Behind the Walls, a project of the Save the Kids, adopts this kind of transformative approach. It does not deal with the issue of sex trafficking, but it does deal with mass incarceration. Legal structures often prohibit both current and former inmates from entering into youth detention centers, and current prisoners are often prohibited from corresponding with detained youth. We believe that this inhibits personal and social transformation. Detained youth can learn a lot from those who have served in adult jails and prisons— what to do and not to do, why and how to avoid the same choices, and how to develop a better personal outlook on life. Likewise, we believe that the youth can provide hope, guidance, and direction for the adults. Wisdom Behind the Walls has thus created a website in which adult prisoners can post various types of writings. A related project, Poetry Behind the Walls, allows detained youth to post poetry. In both cases, we believe that such expression and sharing facilitates cross-generational connection and acts like a transformative tool for all those involved. We believe that this is a healthier and more productive approach to prison life than, say, longer sentences, solitary confinement, or restriction of visitation rights. In no way do such punishments equal transformation.[9]

Thinking about Alternatives

Prisons, guns, armed guards, and punitive approaches are not solutions for building a better world. Instead, we must start developing *skills* and *alternative systems*. By skills, we mean the ability to communicate, actively listen, build groups and teams of mutual support and understanding, forgive ourselves and others, and develop methods for positively transforming those who have hurt others. These skills must then become core practices in our communities, homes, schools, relationships, and places of work. To do this, we need workshops, trainings, and education on the topics of peacemaking and social justice. Everyone must become involved—politicians, teachers, administrators, students, parents, and workers of all levels.

We must also develop new systems that replace the oppressive systems we currently have in place. Some alternative systems might include peer mediation programs in the workplace and school, community dialogues around difficult and controversial topics, and more community-based conflict transformation centers that are free and open to the public. If we can accomplish all of this, then perhaps one day we can forego the need to call police and armed guards, walk around with assault weapons, or build more prisons to house more people.

The Nature of Conflict

All of this comes down to dealing with conflict in positive, helpful, and transformative ways. But before we can begin devising methods for *dealing with* conflict, we should first understand the *nature of* conflict. That begins with realizing that conflict is a *complex* and *daily* experience. We all experience conflict every day—deciding where to eat with friends, hassling with your cell phone provider, arguing with a professor over a grade, explaining to a police officer why you *had* to speed, and working through emotional issues with your romantic partner. These are pretty low-key conflicts. More intense conflicts might involve fistfights, gang violence, and international war. Regardless of the intensity and severity, each conflict involves a plethora of issues—for instance, the wants and needs of each person/party, the social roles that are being enacted, the amount of time needed to hash out the problem, the emotional baggage that we bring to the issue, and the fear and insecurity around "losing face."

The diagram below, entitled "Elements of a Conflict," illustrates five basic elements that are common to every conflict. The first element is a *relationship*, which could be mutual, oppressive, abusive, romantic, professional, or casual. The second element is the *topic* (or issue) that people are arguing over. The third element is the *process* of how the conflict has developed—its history, what people did and said, what is occurring right now.[10]

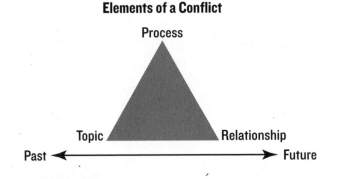

Elements of a Conflict

Process

Topic

Relationship

Past ← → Future

Dealing with Conflict

Ron Claassen, a professor in the Center for Peacemaking and Conflict Studies at Fresno Pacific University, designed a diagram that shows four methods of addressing a conflict.[11] The circle represents the individual(s) who control(s) the decision. In Option #1, one of the individuals has control of the decision, while the other does not, such as in the case of a police officer and a suspect, a teacher and a student, a boss and an employee, or a parent and a child. In Option #2, the control of the decision lies with an outside person or group—this could be a court judge listening to a prosecutor and defendant, a referee between two athletes, a parent between two children, or a teacher between two students. In Option #3, the control of the decision lies with those who are directly involved with the conflict, but there is an external person or group, such as a mediator or facilitator, that makes sure that the conflict moves forward in a constructive manner. Finally, in Option #4, the power lies solely with those involved in the conflict. This could mean two individuals locked in a prison cell fighting over who gets the top bunk, a romantic couple arguing at home over bills, or a community all

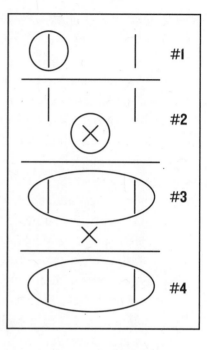

working together at a town hall meeting about ending gun violence. If possible, in our opinion, Option #4 should be used since it allows those who are directly affected by the conflict to work through the issue. But this may not always be possible or even desirable. The people may not have the correct skills to deal with the conflict; one or both parties may have a hidden agenda and thus seek to manipulate the other; and there can be power differentials—police officer and civilian, teacher and student, boss and employee. In these and other cases, it may be necessary to use one of the other options.

Conflict Management and Conflict Resolution: Helpful, but Not Good Enough

Two of the most well-known alternative approaches to conflict are conflict management and conflict resolution. Both methods contribute to building a better world, but unfortunately both also fall short. The biggest problem with these two methods is that they do not sufficiently engage the world of activism and hands-on social change. This is also true with the general field of peace and conflict studies, which has become somewhat removed from actual activism—it's become more of an academic discourse than an actual means to peace activism and organizing. Furthermore, conflict management and resolution have become incorporated into law schools and business administration departments. On the one hand, this is a positive sign of progress. But on the other hand, it has drained these methods of their heart and soul. Conflict management and resolution have become quick methods for resolving disputes over legal contracts—people avoid the court system, and mediators and arbitrators are the new peacemakers. In the business world, conflict resolution and management are used as methods for stabilizing the workplace and creating a professional environment. This is obviously important within professional settings because it allows everyone to be efficient and effective in meeting the goals of the agency. But conflict management and resolution become gutted of their healing powers: they are no longer about caring about and respecting those with whom you work; instead, they are reduced to methods for tolerating and dealing with others and, most troubling, managing your work relations so you can do your job and make money for the company.

In terms of *conflict management*, there are five possible approaches that the involved parties can take: (1) coerce, (2) collaborate, (3) cooperate, (4) compromise, and (5) avoid. These approaches are illustrated in the following diagram. The diagram also includes two arrows: a vertical arrow that points upward—the individual will move upward on the diagram the more s/he is interested in the topic/issue of the conflict; and a horizontal arrow that depicts how much an individual values the relationship—the more someone values the relationship, the more that individual will move toward the right of the diagram. Ideally, all parties to a conflict would have great interest in the topic and truly

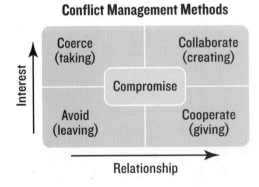

Conflict Management Methods

Interest

Coerce (taking)   Collaborate (creating)

Compromise

Avoid (leaving)   Cooperate (giving)

Relationship

value the relationship. This would enable them to use the collaborative method of managing the conflict. The purpose of collaboration is for *both parties to actively work together* (to the best of their abilities) in coming to a resolution that satisfies everyone.

Conflict resolution is commonly practiced in such professional settings as nonprofits, businesses, and the government. This method revolves around four possible outcomes: (1) both parties win; (2) party A wins while party B loses; (3) party B wins while party A loses; and (4) both parties lose. This method is good for trying to highlight the benefits of achieving a win-win scenario—everyone can walk away feeling good about the outcome. When people know this going into the resolution process, they can be more confident that conflict can be a positive experience. But there is still a major problem with the *conflict resolution model*: it is concerned with the end result and not the process. This model views conflict not as an opportunity for mutual growth and healing, but rather as a problem that needs to be solved and ended. The conflict resolution model is therefore based on conclusion rather than process, on results rather than growth and transformation.

Four Conflict Resolution Outcomes

1. Win – Win
2. Win – Lose
3. Lose – Win
4. Lose – Lose

Restorative Justice: Closer, but Not Quite

Restorative justice is another approach to conflict. In contrast to criminal justice, where you "bring the criminal to justice," this approach seeks to *restore justice* to both the victim and the offender. Restorative justice is based on *voluntary mediation* between victim and offender, revolves around a desire for *healing and forgiveness*, and asks that everyone take some form of *accountability*—this includes the offender, the victim, and the overall community. Ron Claassen, author of *Restorative Justice—Fundamental Principles*, writes the following points about restorative justice:

1. Crime is primarily an offense against human relationships, and secondarily a violation of a law (since laws are written to protect safety and fairness in human relationships).

2. Restorative justice recognizes that crime (violation of persons and relationships) is wrong and should not occur, and also recognizes that after it does there are dangers and opportunities. The danger is that the community, victim(s), and/or offender emerge from the response further alienated, more damaged, disrespected, disempowered, feeling less safe and less cooperative with society. The opportunity is that injustice is recognized, the equity is restored (restitution and grace), and the future is clarified so that participants are safer, more respectful, and more empowered and cooperative with each other and society.

3. Restorative justice is a process to "make things as right as possible" which includes: attending to needs created by the offense, such as safety and repair of injuries to relationships and physical damage resulting from the offense; and attending to needs related to the cause of the offense (addictions, lack of social or employment skills or resources, lack of moral or ethical base, etc.).

4. The primary victim(s) of a crime is/are the one(s) most impacted by the offense. The secondary victims are others impacted by the crime and might include family members, friends, witnesses, criminal justice officials, community, etc.

5. As soon as immediate victim, community, and offender safety concerns are satisfied, restorative justice views the situation as a teachable moment for the offender—an opportunity to encourage the offender to learn new ways of acting and being in community.

6. Restorative justice prefers responding to the crime at the earliest point possible and with the maximum amount of voluntary cooperation and minimum coercion, since healing in relationships and new learning are voluntary and cooperative processes.

7. Restorative justice prefers that most crimes are handled using a cooperative structure, including those impacted by the offense, as a community, to provide support and accountability. This might include primary and secondary victims and family (or substitutes if they choose not to participate), the offender and family, community representatives, government representatives, faith community representatives, school representatives, etc.

8. Restorative justice recognizes that not all offenders will choose to be cooperative. Therefore, there is a need for outside authority to make decisions for the offender who is not cooperative. The actions of the authorities and the consequences imposed should be tested by whether they are reasonable, restorative, and respectful (for victim(s), offender, and community).

9. Restorative justice prefers that offenders who pose significant safety risks and are not yet cooperative be placed in settings where the emphasis is on safety, values, ethics, responsibility, accountability, and civility. They should be exposed to the impact of their crime(s) on victims, invited to learn empathy, and offered learning opportunities to become better equipped with skills to be a productive member of society. They should continually be invited (not coerced) to become cooperative with the community and be given the opportunity to demonstrate this in appropriate settings as soon as possible.

10. Restorative justice requires follow-up and accountability structures utilizing the natural community as much as possible, since keeping agreements is the key to building a trusting community.

11. Restorative justice recognizes and encourages the role of community institutions, including the religious/faith community, in teaching and establishing the moral and ethical standards which build up the community.[12]

These are very admirable qualities and practices. But, strangely, restorative justice does not necessarily address issues of oppression, injustice, and social inequity within conflicts. While restorative justice challenges the retributive justice system and brings people voluntarily together, it fails to recognize the social, political, and economic issues that affect each and every conflict.[13] Conflicts must be seen as opportunities not only to resolve particular problems, but to also resolve injustices that might have fostered the problem. Moreover, restorative implies a restoring back to the way things were, which might imply a state of poverty, slavery, or legalized rape. As can be seen, not everything that existed in the past is good and just. And that is why we turn to transformative justice in the following section.

Transformative Justice: The Right Method for Building a Movement

In recent years many radical justice activists within the US have moved to adopting transformative justice, which builds off the principles and philosophy of restorative justice, while also addressing and challenging systems of oppression, inequity, and domination. It takes a systems approach to conflict, recognizing our interconnections: the offender and the victim; one's choices and one's situation; the community and the social structures; and power differentials among all those involved. Transformative justice argues that we are all involved in complex relationships of oppressors and oppressed, dominators and dominated.[14] We may be the oppressed in one situation, but we may be the oppressor in another situation. We may be the victim from one perspective, but we may be the offender from another perspective. Transformative justice is not about destroying and building anew, and it's not about creating win-lose solutions common to social revolutions in which the oppressed become the new oppressors.[15] Instead, transformative justice asks that *everyone* and *everything* change—we as individuals, as well as our systems, structures, and relationships.

Transformative justice addresses not only the specific conflict between victim and offenders, but also the plethora of social issues that come to bear on that conflict. For instance, a 14-year-old boy, who is from a poor neighborhood and identifies as queer, robs a store at 2:00 AM. Transformative justice looks not only at the crime of burglary, but also at why the boy committed the act. Was the boy kicked out of his home by a father who was homophobic? Was the boy needing money for food, clothes, or a place to stay? Was he trying to get money to help his younger sister who also is homeless? These questions are addressed in order to understand the whole context, which, unfortunately, involves a great deal of injustice. Our society oppresses and marginalizes those who are poor and queer. Consequently, there are two victims within this scenario—the store owner who was robbed, and the 14-year-old boy who is a victim of wider systemic injustice. This is a clear example of how the systems approach of transformative justice breaks down common barriers between victim and offender, creates a much wider understanding of abuse and violence, and tries to bring everyone together in a transformative relationship.[16]

Social justice activists often identify the oppressor as the enemy. While this is understandable, transformative justice actually challenges this perspective: no one is an enemy; instead, everyone needs to be involved in a voluntary, safe, constructive, and critical dialogue about accountability, responsibility, and the initiative to heal. This means that both activists and oppressors, as well as law enforcement, lawyers, judges, prisoners, community members, teachers, students, politicians, spiritual leaders, and others, must come together. It is for this reason that we should be willing to work with a diversity of people in our push for a better world. Transformative justice looks for the good in others, while also acknowledging the complex systems that we all live within.

Below are 10 general principles of transformative justice. These will hopefully help to crystalize what has been said thus far.

1. Transformative justice stresses the notion that the *current criminal justice system in the US separates the victim and the offender.* This re-victimizes the victim by granting the government control over the decision-making process and it changes the offender into a victim of the state by inflicting punishment rather than education or rehabilitation.
2. Transformative justice is based on *prison abolition.*
3. Transformative justice brings issues of identity into the realm of justice by *addressing socio-political injustices* toward women, people of color, LGBTQ people, poor people, immigrants, people with disabilities, and other oppressed and marginalized groups.
4. Transformative justice believes that *"crime" is framed by the state* and not by the community.
5. Transformative justice believes in *de-institutionalization,* empowering people rather than institutions to make decisions.
6. Transformative justice is *against violence and punishment.*

7. Transformative justice believes in the value of *mediation, negotiation, and community* to transform conflicts.

8. Transformative justice *values conflict as an opportunity for growth,* progress, and social justice.

9. Transformative justice identifies *crime as conflict.* "Crime" is an institutionalized term used by government to describe conflict. It is a term to conjure harm (rather than opportunity, which is the case of conflict), and constructs the binary of victim versus offender.

10. Transformative justice is for *total liberation* and the end of all systems of domination.

These 10 principles are only a beginning. They must be challenged, extended, critiqued, and redeveloped by peace workers, penal abolitionists, social justice activists, and those from oppressed communities, especially those incarcerated. Transformative justice is therefore open to revision and is adaptable to social changes. The point is to open ourselves up to perpetual progress and justice. To help us enact this processual goal, we have outlined eight steps for dealing with conflict in a transformative manner.

1. *Critically reflect* on your own assumptions, judgments, behaviors, choice of words, and social, economic, and political positioning.

2. *Take accountability* for your actions, both personally and publicly. Usually, this means acknowledging your culpability to yourself and others.

3. *Take responsibility* to work to end future injustices and oppressions that can be caused within both interpersonal and social contexts.

4. *Understand* that when they are in a conflict, most people are not taught how to love themselves or others. Instead, they are often taught to defend themselves and to attack others verbally and/or physically.

5. Given our current social world, it is also important to *avoid attacking others publicly* via the Internet (e.g., websites, Facebook, Twitter, blogs). Once a comment is posted, the whole world is able to repost it, and it is difficult to remove the comment.

6. When possible, *limit indirect communication* (passing messages through a third party), which can often involve a lot of misinterpretation. Instead, try to develop opportunities to communicate in person. If face-to-face is not possible, then phone, Skype, text, email, and other forms of private communication can be used, and, if necessary, recorded, videoed, copy/pasted, and forwarded.

7. Be aware of and be able to *navigate culturally based conflicts.* Cultural differences should be acknowledged and respected—for example, religion, language, food, art, expression, and education. This also involves historical cultural context, such as colonialism, imperialism, genocide, war, and the influence of geographical region.

8. Strive to *include rather than exclude* others for their wrongdoing. It usually helps to separate the wrongful action from the person's humanity. The person should not be defined by his or her wrongful actions. This helps to forgive and to heal.

Conclusion: Transformation, Not Escalation

Transformative justice, unlike restorative justice or conflict management and resolution, seeks to challenge all aspects of authoritarianism, domination, oppression, and control within society. For this reason, transformative justice is more than an alternative approach to conflict or to the criminal justice system. Instead, it is a nondogmatic, process-oriented social justice philosophy for peace that allows for creative approaches in transforming conflict and addressing issues of brutality, assault, abuse, victimization, accountability, responsibility, loss, and healing.[17]

We have been involved with numerous organizations, collectives, affinity groups, movements, support committees, and projects, and we know firsthand that achieving transformation is *extremely difficult.* One of the biggest barriers to transformation is escalation—when a small conflict quickly escalates to a larger conflict. At that point, both sides dig in and refuse to give in. This experience is illustrated in the diagram below, "Behaviors of Escalation within Conflict." As the large arrow rises upward, conflict escalates and moves farther away from peace and closer to violence. One of the biggest contributors to this escalation is a lack of trust. We are more prone to escalate toward anger and violence if we do not trust one another. Fearing that the other person will harm us (physically, emotionally, or socially), we subconsciously jump ahead, as if to harm the other first. According to the model, this experience involves seven potential stages, beginning with a peaceful state and ending with a violent state.

We should realize that we do not necessarily or literally exist in a "state of peace." Instead, we are experientially aware of how our minds and bodies feel in each of these stages—there is a bodily difference between, for example, peace and irritation. Developing a more mindful awareness of these emotional states can help us *avoid* escalation. We can further avoid escalation by (1) recognizing that there is no one correct outcome to the conflict; (2) learning to talk less and to actively listen; (3) being honest about our feelings, but also being able to communicate those feelings in non-defensive and non-accusatory ways; and (4) maintaining that each person is a complex being influenced by a plethora of factors, many of which we are unaware of. As can be seen, none of this is easy, and most of it starts with you as an individual. As a peace activist, you must be committed to transforming yourself in order to transform the world.

Behaviors of Escalation Within Conflict

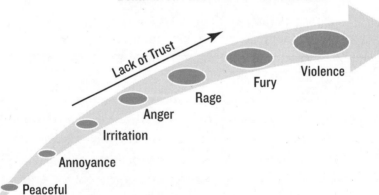

Lack of Trust

Violence

Fury

Rage

Anger

Irritation

Annoyance

Peaceful

PART 3

GETTING INTO THE STREETS

5

Organizing Your Community

DREW ROBERT WINTER

At this stage of history, either one of two things is possible. Either the general population will take control of its own destiny and will concern itself with community interests guided by values of solidarity and sympathy and concern for others, or, alternatively, there will be no destiny for anyone to control.

— NOAM CHOMSKY

PEOPLE ARE THE BASIS OF DEMOCRACY, SO IF YOU WANT DE-mocracy, you need people. You can write a touching poem or book, know every fact in the world about who is suffering under which system of oppression, and have an encyclopedia of proposed policy solutions and theories of justice. But none of those is meaningful unless there are people behind it. An idea without a body to occupy it is nothing; it couldn't even exist. But once it enters the body it begins to impact time and space in potentially revolutionary ways. If it's the right idea, it will not only be correct in theory, but will replicate itself and spread. Organizing is not an exact science; lots can go wrong, and things can always be done differently. But folks who are keen and passionate do not need road signs when there are paths that have been formed by others who have already traveled. What follows are some general insights, observations, and suggestions that can be helpful in transforming isolated individuals into an empowered community capable of fighting for social change.

Organizing vs. Activism

Although the terms "organizing" and "activism" are often considered synonymous, there are important distinctions. Organizing is about developing a large number of individuals with aligned (although not necessarily identical) goals, and enabling the various types of individuals and motivations to act as a unified front for social change. Organizing can begin with as little as one person, but usually, it is a few motivated, brave, and forward-thinking individuals. From this nucleus, an infrastructure is built that will recruit more and more people, and, hopefully, over time, the organization that you are building will take on a life of its own.

Organizing is the necessary prelude to large-scale activism. Activism is the campaign to win a long-term battle, but organizing builds the means to fight it.[1] The use of "battle" may seem like a militant analogy, but it is important to understand that all justice work that is effective inevitably has an opposition. And, most likely, that opposition is causing significant suffering and inequality. Rallying for better schools means colliding with those who do not want to reallocate funds for schools. Organizing an anti-war protest means facing down the war machine. Marching against racism means confronting racists. And so on and so on. Activism and organizing imply battles and struggles. These battles do not have to be violent, but they are oppositional and confrontational.

Understanding People, Power, and Psychology

The same knowledge required of an activist in order to understand persuasion on an individual level is required of an organizer in order to persuade a larger constituency or a general demographic. You are often applying that knowledge at a broad, long-term level to "types" of individuals as you shape your plan for organizing. For instance, individuals tend to have a bias toward the status quo, meaning that you should attempt to shape your message in a way that appeals to your target's perception of what's socially normal. This should come through not only in your message, but in how you present yourself. At the very least, this means dressing in attire that's similar to your target audience; if you are ever in doubt, then dress more conservatively than your target audience, as this makes you look more professional to a wider variety of people. Try to use words, phrases, or signs that already carry weight with those people you seek to have on your side. For example, the American flag as a symbol is often used to justify a great number of social and political actions precisely because of its power in appealing to nationalist sentiments. If your campaign centers around a school tuition increase, for example, you might consider utilizing the school's mascot, or re-writing of a popular sports chant, to connect with students. This will make people in your community identify with the problem, which is the key to persuading them to attend protests or sit-ins, write letters, or attend sign-making parties. Obviously, you cannot appeal to every segment of the population in every way—if you could, you probably wouldn't need to be organizing in the first place. Ideally, you want to market your message and your organization in a way that is appealing to your target audience and is minimally hostile to segments of the population you don't intend to win over. For example, if you are a student attempting to get more vegan options in your school cafeteria, then appealing to students will be ideal. That's because they can potentially identify with you, and they are the largest demographic within this population (as opposed to, say, teachers or administrators). Your organization/group should also have a public face of that demographic (i.e., a student that others can relate to). You should also try to avoid appearing too "anti-tradition," which might offend and alienate the school's administration and staff, who are likely older and more conservative.

But realize that there are some differences between institutions and individuals. Although institutions comprise individuals who respond to rhetorical and emotional tactics, their behaviors are bound by external forces that require more than simple persuasion and charm to overcome. But the good news is that institutions *do* re-spond to blunt, sustained pressure, whereas individuals usually feel alienated and shut you out. Institutions cannot simply walk away from you and throw your leaflet in the garbage; they exist, by defini-tion, in a fixed position within society and hence must face the waves of public opposition head on. Whether their office walls will fend off your demands will depend on the force and pressure you can muster. The trick is to find and then repeatedly pressure the weak point(s). Hopefully, you will be able to use some of the institution's own assets and tools against itself. If the institution is a school administration, you may be able to persuade alumni (donors to the school) that the administration's position makes the school look bad, so they will pressure the administration themselves; alumni have both social and financial capital for the school, so their opinion matters to admin-istration. You could look for contradictions in the institution's own policies, whether they are codes of conduct or municipal ordinances. You could also give former employees a chance to speak out about wrongdoing they witnessed—many campaigns start because of testi-monies from former employees who were fired for reporting abuses to their bosses. But never underestimate the opposition—they prob-ably have much experience in dealing with activists, and organizers must be able to think on their feet in order to outmaneuver and stay one step ahead. Like all battle plans, yours must be flexible enough to adapt to frequent, rapid changes as the campaign unfolds, but be strong and clear enough that people never forget who you are and what you are fighting for.

The First Step

A social campaign begins when someone defines a problem and acts to solve that problem by appealing to members of society. An orga-nizer understands that substantive action can come only from many individuals working together. To maximize your abilities, you should first seek out those other individuals as motivated as you through whatever means possible: hang flyers in places where people who share your beliefs are likely to be; create a Facebook page open to the public; begin a reading group at a local bookstore; create an online meetup; write letters to the editor of the local newspaper; talk to your friends, family, and those around you about what you believe to be a serious issue. Many people may agree with you that issue X is a problem, but few will express serious interest in building a sustained movement. But you will likely find a few others who are just as concerned as you and who have the time, resources, and motivation to make it their focus and to build a coalition to accomplish the task.

At the outset, this core group will be your entire organization and will make the critical decisions regarding how to proceed. The initial decisions are:

- What is the *specific issue* that we are concerned about?
- *Who else* in the community is concerned, and what trait(s) do they have in common?
- What is our *proposed solution* to the problem?
- If the community is not concerned, how do we *persuade* them? Or, are we off track?

The last point is important. If you are the only one concerned about an issue and yet you want to devote your entire existence to solving it, then you are clearly out of step with those you need in order to accomplish your goal. If that's true, then maybe your goal is incorrect. This is especially important if you are not a longstanding member of the community. People of different genders, races, and classes may have very different needs and problems; they might also have different feelings about political issues. Suppose, for example, that you want to impose limits on how long a dog may be left outside on a chain. This concern may resonate with people who already don't leave their dogs outside for long periods. But this same issue would be actively opposed by communities where leaving a dog outside on a chain is normal. If you are contemplating such a campaign, it would be advisable to think about whether you want to pull together a coalition of outsiders and powerbrokers to institute a law, or if there are other, more pressing issues in this community—e.g., reducing the number of home foreclosures or even reducing the cost of the weekly trash pickup. One of these issues might garner far more support from the overall community, which may then put you in a more favorable position to discuss the issue of animal welfare at a later time.

"Unite the Divided, Divide the United"

The main rule of organizing is to unite your allies and divide your opposition. When considering those who would be interested in your cause, it is imperative that you understand the many reasons why someone would want to take your side on the issue. Perhaps you are attempting to prevent Walmart from coming to your town, and perhaps a local real-estate developer is angry at the city council for denying him a building permit in the place where Walmart wants to build a new store. Getting this developer's alliance can help you revoke Walmart's permit to build. He needn't ally himself directly with your organization nor hold any moral precepts about the rapacious effects of corporate capitalism; he only needs to be a third party who will support your end goal, while garnering support from many other small business owners who might otherwise cringe at being associated with an "activist" organization.

Some reasons why someone might be interested in a cause include:

- *Financial* interest.
- Feeling *empowered*.
- Being part of a *community*.
- Feeling like a *good person*.
- A *past incident* that creates emotional sensitivity to the issue.
- Deeply held *beliefs* (ethical, religious, political).

"Deeply held beliefs" is intentionally placed at the bottom since, statistically, the number of people who actually join your cause for a sustained period based on this reason alone will be very low: more than simply an abstract notion of right and wrong is necessary to create a *motivated* individual. Financial interest is at the top because it is a very tangible, real form of self-interest that can be extremely motivating. This need not be a bad thing: students protesting tuition increases—particularly at schools made up of more middle- and working-class students—have a very legitimate reason to protest and also a very real financial interest that will get them to your events to kick up a fuss. What's important is to be mindful of both the advantages and limitations of every motivation. People committed to your cause because of financial interest will leave when they no longer have a financial interest at stake. This could be exploited by your opposition in the form of grandfathering in students to keep lower tuition rates. You will therefore want to try, when possible, to shape an end goal so that it is less costly for your opposition to concede than to pay the cost of bribing (in one way or another) large demographics of your support with half-measures and symbolic gestures, as so often happens.

Recruiting Members

There are two primary ways to recruit members: mass marketing and individual appeals. A good organization should be able to do both, and the two will often overlap.

Mass Marketing

Mass marketing is any attempt to recruit many individuals at the same time. This can be achieved by posting flyers, and by advertising in public areas and at events—parks, coffee shops, bookstores, conferences, concerts, university commons, and campus organization fairs are excellent venues. When you are attempting to recruit like this, you need to have a quick, enticing pitch that will find its way into the consciousness of a population that—in the age of texting and Twitter—is plagued by a remarkably short attention span. Your pitch should include one or (at most) two sentences describing the purpose and methods of your group in a way that appeals to your target audience. Additionally, you should be able to provide important logistical information on how people can get involved. For instance, if you are recruiting people at an organization fair or on a street corner, you could have a two-sentence verbal pitch memorized, and then hand out a small flyer. The flyer might have some text encapsulating your group's ideas, but also your group's meeting time and location, directions on how to get there, where to park, how to enter the building, and how to get to the correct room. Any confusion whatsoever will greatly reduce the likelihood of attendance. Contact information for questions is also vital, and normally includes an email address and/or phone number. Be sure to always respond to emails as soon as possible, answer your phone in a professional manner, and promptly return missed calls.

Mass marketing is very effective for recruiting people who are wary of being asked to make a commitment on the spot. Mass marketing allows these people to make a very small time investment and decide on their own terms whether they would like to get more involved. Signing up for an email list or taking a flyer doesn't put any initial responsibility on people, but allows them to consider joining, whereas a direct request might have scared them off.

One-on-One

Speaking directly to individuals places more emphasis on personal relationships and— especially in the early stages of building a campaign—can be vital for bringing in people who will have responsibility and a greater level of commitment. This may be done by systematically going door to door or by simply reaching out to those you know in the community. When you have an extended conversation with someone, you have the opportunity for really getting to know that person's fears, passions, motivations, strengths, and weaknesses. But in order to know these things, you must listen. Hear what others have to say, and keep your own contributions to the conversation at a minimum. People like to talk, especially about themselves, and they therefore tend to like people who let them do that. Find out what kind of interests they have, and what you can offer them. Do they have a set of talents you need? Do they enjoy research? Are they just looking for something to put on a résumé or CV? Are they worried about the education system? Do they fear for the future of their children? Do they care about animals or the environment? Find out their parameters for getting involved, and try to find a place for them to fit into your campaign or organization.

One method of recruitment that blends mass marketing and one-on-one interaction is tabling—literally putting a table in an area with a lot of foot traffic and offering information about your group. This creates an available space that will offer both the low-commitment materials (flyers, an email sign-up sheet) and the possibility for individual or small group conversation. Tabling may require a permit, but this should be relatively easy to obtain. When tabling, make sure that the table is occupied by group members who are capable of speaking to strangers and responding to common questions from both potential allies *and* potential enemies. This latter ability is important since you want to minimize the hostility that might result from a confrontation with people who oppose your cause and/or politics. You want to light a fire under your allies while pacifying your opposition.

Maintaining Membership and Delegating Responsibility

As most organizers quickly discover, a small percentage of those who sign up for an email list or grab a flyer will actually turn up at events, and an even smaller percentage will become permanently active members. But there are ways to maximize the possibility that they will turn up and return.

Every successful organization must:

- Be *effective.*
- Be *interesting.*
- Be *well-organized.*
- *Rely on its members* to be these things.

Your organization or campaign must involve each member. Otherwise, the members are merely spectators. A spectator has no more of a role in the unfolding of your cause than s/he does in the unfolding of a tennis match. Being a spectator doesn't require anything; spectators are therefore less likely to attend meetings, contribute ideas, and dedicate time to accomplishing the group's goals. Your job is to turn people from spectators into members who are willing to work for the cause and become part of a wider community. People who are committed to a cause or group are committed because they feel that they have a necessary role to play. This is an important point because organizers are notorious for their desire to get things done, and that often means doing things themselves. But organizing is not about one individual getting things done; it's about creating an empowered community capable of acting as cohesive unit. As the saying goes, "Don't do for others what they can do for themselves."

Giving people responsibility gives them purpose and pressures them to come through since others are counting on them. If they fail, they risk losing face, feeling devalued, or even being alienated from the group. Obviously, you don't want to give a stranger a large responsibility just to try to bring her or him into the group. But assigning people responsibilities is not only necessary for large events to take place; it also serves as a litmus test for people's level of trust, leadership, and accomplishment. Can you count on them for getting things done? It doesn't make them bad people if they can't be relied upon, but you need to know one way or the other before they are assigned major tasks (e.g., launching a website, talking with elected officials, raising funds, drafting proposals).

When you are initially organizing, divide up responsibilities for a small event, such as a potluck. Ask everyone to bring specific items— pens and paper, fruit juice, soft drinks, plates and utensils. Those who arrive on time and with the requested items will give you an initial indication of where responsibility can be placed. Over time, responsibility should end up in the hands of everyone who wants it and can be counted upon to utilize it—your own skills and leadership should, over time, be less and less central to the group functioning. Ideally, others will become confident and empowered enough that you will become just another member of the group.

Garnering Wider Support

The few people you meet at the beginning of your campaign will most likely form the core of your group and become the main organizers. But you will come across many more people who will exhibit marginal or sporadic interest based on their mood and personal issues and circumstances. You cannot assume that you will have vast legions of activists and organizers standing shoulder to shoulder. While that is possible (think of all the millions of people who participate in major social movements), it's unlikely for a small, localized group and campaign. It is therefore incumbent upon you to maximize the participation of those who are dedicated and committed, while *also* garnering wider support from sympathetic allies. These allies might not come to meetings and help with hands-on tasks, but they might attend protests, provide a few pithy and supportive quotes to reporters, and help spread a sense of righteousness throughout the wider community. Achieving this kind of wider support is very important, as it can create a "buzz" around your campaign, raise awareness about your issue in an implicit, diffuse manner, and infuse some fun into your daily organizing efforts. No one likes to play for a losing team. But a team with energy and support can make the effort worthwhile, which potentially attracts even more supporters. As the well-known 20th-century organizer Saul Alinsky once observed, a "good tactic is one your people enjoy. If your people are not having a ball doing it, there is something very wrong with the tactic."

These insights have played themselves out in my own organizing efforts. For instance, when I was in college I was the president of the school's animal rights group. Every week we had four to eight people attend our meetings, during which we planned and evaluated campaigns. Of the four to eight who attended, only four attended consistently, and those individuals (including myself) were the driving force of the organization. However, with the work of just the four of us, we were able to organize a campaign against the animal circus that came to the school every year, and our campaign culminated in over 80 students attending a protest that attracted citywide news coverage. The circus became a major issue, with letters, news articles, and opinion pieces regularly published in all the local print media. Comments—both for and against our group—characterized us as though we were a powerful nonprofit organization with a staff and a vast following. We did have some initial student support, but the growth of debate convinced large portions of the public that we were indeed very organized, and that perception led to a level of support so high that the school board of trustees prevented the circus from returning the following year. This occurred because four dedicated students skillfully crafted and disseminated a message, spoke with authority, and organized less interested individuals to make their voices heard in the public sphere through carefully timed protest and engagement with news media.

We knew that our largest base of support would be the student body. We painted the issue as a matter of the university being "behind the times" by allowing such an event. By painting the circus as a conservative institution from an earlier, less civilized time, we were able to win over a large swath of young people. This is also the demographic that, statistically, is most sensitive to issues of animal cruelty. Protesting the circus, therefore, made students feel like they were actually standing up for their school and the values it *ought to* represent. This was more effective than a campaign focused on, say, boycotting the circus, since virtually no students attended anyway—attendees were mostly working-class families with neither political sway over the university administration nor (broadly speaking) the same priority of concern for animals in circuses as the student body. If we had chosen a tactic that required students to do more, such as occupying the administration building during early-morning meetings, the vast majority who attended the 2:00 p.m. protest would likely still have been asleep, and the occupation—if it had any chance at all—would have been characterized as a small group of militant students, and backfired. The key was understanding who our supporters were and what they found manageable and interesting. When a tactic or strategy gets stale to your supporters, consider changing it.

Understanding Limits of Participants

It's often easier for those who lead to make social justice the centerpiece of their lives. After all, making social justice the centerpiece of your life tends to give you opportunities for leadership. But most of the people you will be involved with will not have such a focus. They will likely have other very real responsibilities relating to their careers and families. They may not have a lot of talking points and statistics memorized, or have training in how to effectively speak to the news media. But that's not the point; your goal is a much more modest one. You are simply trying to get people to dedicate small pieces of time and effort. Most people do want to see justice for themselves and others, and that's what you are working on together. But this involves respecting the limitations of participants—they will have jobs to go to, kids to pick up from school, parents to care for, houses to clean, dinners to cook, and friendships to maintain. This is not a license to let people off the hook—your issue should, if it is important, be worthy of significant time and energy. But it will never be quite the same for the core organizers as it is for occasional activists. Organizers start with the goal of committing and have the privilege of planning ahead, while occasional participants are contributing time between other obligations. This should be understood ahead of time so as to not create unrealistic expectations.

Concluding Remarks

What it takes to be an effective organizer has filled thousands of books, pamphlets, and websites. But if nothing else, the brief guidelines listed above should help readers *start* their own groups, organizations, and campaigns. Organizing is not just about accomplishing tasks, but also about creating a sense of solidarity within the community. That community can be among a few friends, or be spread out across a town, city, neighborhood, college campus, or nationwide network. The point is to facilitate a collection of people who are willing and able to fight against the inequality, injustice, and misery that is so pervasive. Taking on such a challenge is never easy, but that means that we, as organizers, must be ever more disciplined, dedicated, and passionate in our push for equality and justice.

Activist Guidelines and Case Studies

JASON DEL GANDIO, JAMES GENERIC, AARON ZELLHOEFER, AND ANTHONY J. NOCELLA II

Never doubt that a small group of thoughtful, committed, citizens can change the world. Indeed, it is the only thing that ever has.

— ATTRIBUTED TO MARGARET MEAD

Get up, stand up, stand up for your rights! Get up, stand up, don't give up the fight!

— BOB MARLEY

Let me hear you say fight the power. We've got to fight the powers that be.

— PUBLIC ENEMY

THIS CHAPTER PROVIDES FOUR SNAPSHOTS OF ACTIVISM. Jason Del Gandio begins with how to initiate and facilitate an organizing meeting. This is usually the first place activists begin—getting together and discussing what needs to be done and how to do it. Jason uses his experience with Occupy Philly's media working group as a running example. In the second snapshot, James Generic provides a narrative about the Wooden Shoe bookstore, which is an all-volunteer, collectively run, and financially viable store based on anarchist principles. James has volunteered at the Shoe for 13 years, and is intimately familiar with its organizational structure, daily operations, and the communal/political space that it provides for activists. The third snapshot is by Aaron Zellhoefer, who worked with the organization Minnesota United for All Families (MUAF). In brief, MUAF trained its volunteers to engage in conversation with friends and family on the issue of same-sex marriage in order to successfully oppose an amendment to the state constitution. The fourth and final snapshot, by Anthony J. Nocella II, focuses on his involvement with the grassroots organization Save the Kids. By relying on the appeal of hip-hop activism and the principles of transformative justice, Save the Kids steers kids away from the prison-industrial complex and toward a life of opportunity and success. These snapshots hopefully provide readers with ideas, strategies, and guidelines for doing their own activism.

Occupy Philly: Starting a Campaign, Facilitating a Meeting   (by Jason Del Gandio)

New activists often ask, "Where do I begin?" You usually begin with a small group of people who want to change something. From there, you have to get others involved. That means setting up an *initial public meeting*. During that meeting you present the problem, issue, or concern and try to persuade the attendees that your proposed change is beneficial to their lives. But you also want to be open to their views, perspectives, and grievances. In many ways, it's about *facilitating a dialogue* and enabling people to *come together* to fight for change.

To demonstrate how this might be done, I am using my experience with the "media working group" from Occupy Philly. Occupy Philly began in early October 2011. (The main occupation, Occupy New York, had begun in September.) Like most occupations, we had numerous working groups that were the core of Occupy Philly. These working groups were open to anyone who wanted to participate—if you were interested in joining a particular group, you attended the meeting and began helping out. The working groups included, but were not limited to: sanitation, food, library, security, entertainment, outreach and public relations, direct action, daycare, art, education, and interfaith. Working groups would meet independently and then designate one person to provide report-backs to the general assembly committee or during the generally assembly. The general assembly (GA) was the main gathering open to the public that would discuss, debate, and make collective decisions. The GA would occur each day at a certain time; all those attending could participate to one degree or another; models of consensus decision-making were used. GAs could be quick and easy, but usually they were long and arduous processes; including everyone's voice is not easy, but that's the nature of direct democracy. This is how most collective decisions were made by Occupy Philly—e.g., whether or not we should seek a city permit, where to place the food station, when and where to march or demonstrate, whether to leave and re-occupy another space or to stand and resist when we were going to be kicked out.

WALL STREET IS OUR STREET!

The media working group would meet once per week, although some members did meet more often. We had an actual "media tent" to keep equipment (laptops, printers, wireless routers, papers) safe and dry. Overall, the media working group sought to *create media*, which focused for the most part on writing stories and creating video and audio content that would be posted on our website.[1] The purpose was to create media by the very people who were participating in Occupy Philly—media by the people and for the people.

So how did the Occupy Philly media working group get started? Someone decided that a media team was necessary and put out a general call during a GA meeting: basically, "Meet me in that corner over there if you want to work on media." People gathered, exchanged names and contact info, and set up regular times and places to meet. It is really as simple as that. However, coordinating people's schedules, accommodating one another's beliefs and ideologies, and agreeing on what to actually do is always complicated. Below, I walk through some steps for facilitating a grassroots meeting. At times,

I will use examples from the Occupy Philly media working group to explicate my points.

Get the Meeting Started

- Do a *go-around* and have people introduce themselves: names, experiences with the issue at hand or with other campaigns, reasons for attending this meeting. But keep it brief; this can take up a *lot* of time if not managed well.
- Choose someone to *facilitate* the meeting. (Someone will usually volunteer; if not, be prepared to volunteer yourself.)
- Ask someone to *take notes*. (Those notes will then be emailed to people.)
- Do you need someone to *write on a board* or large sheets of paper (such as butcher paper or large sketchbooks)?
- Pass around a *sign-in sheet*: ask for name, email, phone number, and affiliation with a particular organization.
- Set a time limit or a specific time to end. This will help keep people focused and give you an excuse to "speed up the process." (Some people like to go off on tangents.)
- The first few meetings will go slowly as folks get to know each other and analyze what needs to be done.

Decide on a Name for the Campaign or Organization

- Try to use a *name that is snappy* and easy to remember. A good acronym is always helpful. Occupy Philly Media (OPM) was used for obvious reasons—it was easy to say and remember and directly explained what we were doing.

What's the Issue (Problem and Solution)?

- If you are the one who is setting up the first meeting, make sure you can *quickly state/summarize the issue*. That includes both the problem and a possible/preliminary solution. For OPM, that was fairly straightforward—to create media for Occupy Philly. But there was still debate and discussion. What should that media look like? Should just anyone be able to write and post a story? Who is going to be the webmaster? Who is going to have access to our Facebook page? Should we try to work with local corporate media? Should we invite "official" reporters and journalists to our meetings, or exclude them? These questions were *not* easily answered.

Who Are Your Potential Allies and Constituents?

- Who has a *natural affiliation* with your campaign? Who will be on your side? What groups and organizations will support you? Does anyone in the room have connections to these other groups?
- OPM sought out folks in Occupy Philly who might be good at creating media. OPM also tried to connect with and write about various *grassroots organizations* that were participating in the occupation. This allowed us to publicize their work and helped bring more traffic to our website. These actions helped us build allies and constituents.

Do You Have Any Enemies?

- Are there any *people/groups that will oppose* and try to stop you? Is there anyone who is naturally against what you are doing? If so, is it worth talking to them, or should you simply ignore them and expect their opposition? Will they try to attack you in the public spotlight (e.g., in the media or at public events)?
- Occupy was already a national campaign that attracted plenty of naysayers, but OPM worked to *combat some of the negative publicity*—to help *shape the Occupy message*.

Who Can Do What?

- What skills does each person have and *how can each person contribute*? Determining this allows everyone to know what the group is currently capable of accomplishing; you may have web designers; journalists; people who can make t-shirts, flyers, or posters; teachers who can talk in public, make mass copies, or obtain office supplies; librarians who can do research or might have good organizational skills; economists who can run numbers; or even deli or grocery-store workers who might be able to get free food.

- OPM actually asked "Who can do what?" at the *start of every meeting* (more or less), so as to better incorporate new attendees and to remind everyone of people's capabilities. OPM was constantly evolving as Occupy itself evolved, so this was actually an important step.

How Much Time Can Folks Dedicate to This Issue/Event/Campaign?

- It is sometimes best to ask this in terms of *hours per week*. This allows you to know how much the group can get done each week, and then guess how long it will take you to get some real things accomplished. You might add this question to your sign-in sheet, or you can just ask it orally: one hour? three hours? five hours? 10 or more hours?
- OPM had a *variety of time commitments*. Some people were in the media tent multiple hours each day. Others put in a few hours a week from home. And others attended the weekly meeting and contributed an hour or two on their own.

Create a Tentative Timeline

- *Long-term goals:* six to 12 months. *Mid-term goals:* three to six months. *Short-term goals:* one week to three months. *Immediate needs:* one day to one week. These time lengths are relative to what you are trying to accomplish. If you are organizing a single demonstration, then you simply need to pick a date and work around that time frame. If you are lobbying Congress to pass or oppose a bill, then you need to know when Congress meets and allow enough time to effectively pressure particular representatives. OPM was structured around immediate and short-term goals since everything was unfolding in the moment.

Designate Working Groups and Ask for Volunteers

- OPM was a working group, but even within this group there were small teams responsible for specific tasks. This involves a *distribution of work*: who is going to do what?

- Most groups, organizations, and campaigns will have *some combination of the following working groups*: research/background info; education/consciousness raising; outreach/coalition building/ recruiting more people; media/communications/literature; website/listserv/social media; the "point person" (the person who takes responsibility for completing a particular task, or even the overall campaign); and scheduling and facilitating meetings.

Background Knowledge/Information Up to this Point

- The lead organizers should have some knowledge about the issue that the group/campaign is addressing and share that knowledge with those who are attending the meeting. The lead organizers should then open up the floor to everyone, asking the attendees if they have more knowledge/information. Who knows what? For OPM, this sharing of knowledge was more of a skills issue—who can do what? But knowledge was still important. How do we set up an Internet connection in a public space? How much will it cost? What are some of the major stories that we should start writing about immediately? In general, *knowledge is your friend*— the more you know and the sooner you know it, the better your campaign will be.

Any Other Points of Business?

- Always make room for *a few issues at the end* that people want to raise. But be careful—some people will use that time for no good reason. Be sure to keep it all focused.

Set the Next Meeting

- Set the time, the location, and, if known, the focus of the next meeting.
- Then send out a follow-up email within a day or two that thanks everyone for coming and includes the information about the next meeting.
- Also send out an email a couple of days before the next meeting to remind everyone.

Not all of the above steps will be necessary during your first public meeting. But always plan ahead and think about what that initial meeting will need in order to start a successful campaign. Once the campaign starts, keep it up and keep moving forward.

The Wooden Shoe: Running an All-Volunteer Collective Bookstore   (by James Generic)

The Wooden Shoe is an anarchist bookstore collective in Philadelphia that carries radical literature and paraphernalia, offers free political events and meeting space, and is a social space for radicals in the city—for those who have long been engaged and for the newly politicized. It was founded in 1976 by a group of activists coming out of the experience of the 1960s–'70s who were looking for a tangible organization that would operate permanently. More than 35 years later, the Wooden Shoe continues to be a beacon of reliability. It operates as a space where anyone can pop in and learn about what is happening in the city politically, educate her/himself on a particular subject, or simply have a conversation with some other like-minded people. In this society, which is incredibly alienating and hyper-individualized, the simple act of providing a reliable source of information in a live setting is very powerful. Also, and just as importantly, the ability to plug into this kind of organization makes the Wooden Shoe a valuable way for young people, newly politicized people, or people new to Philadelphia to become involved in radical networks and organizations.

We are open seven days a week, from noon to 10:00 PM. Keeping these hours is important because it demonstrates that such an all-volunteer organization can indeed keep to its mission *and* keep itself financially viable. We have all kinds of books on all kinds of topics: history, theory, ideas for action, current events, radical fiction, art, education, race, gender, sexuality, class, economics, and a whole lot more. We've got zines, music, movies, patches, stickers, buttons, and posters. We have free Internet access. We do regular author events, speaker events, and reading groups. We offer group meeting space, and have done support for other radical activist groups in the city, such as giving groups money when we have it. We operate as a collective of over 40 people, with different levels of commitment, almost all of whom have other jobs or are in school. The efforts of the people in the collective make this space viable.

Incorporating New Members

The Wooden Shoe tries to bring new people along slowly. My experience is that every organization has an inner circle of people who tend to direct the course of that organization, and the trick is not to pretend that you don't; instead, have a process for new people to become part of that "inner circle" rather than leaving them to just get to know the right people.[2] Once you have established yourself as an organization, particularly one that runs a continuous operation, you must be honest about your expectations of the members of the organization—particularly be aware that there will be different levels of commitment. In a really loose organization, for instance, you'll see that high levels of activity will not be very sustainable, with sharp highs and lows. Within such an organization, only a select group of people know what is happening, and the burden of everyday operations falls on them.

The Wooden Shoe is an all-volunteer, collectively run Infoshop located in Philadelphia, Pennsylvania, that seeks to embody the principles of anarchism and other movements for social justice. We strive to provide our local community with radical and non-traditional sources of written, digital, and spoken information. We wish to be an empowering resource for activism, organizing, art, self-education, dialogue, community-building, and the anti-capitalist struggle.
— WOODEN SHOE MISSION STATEMENT, MARCH 2009

At the Wooden Shoe, based on a model we borrowed from the Red Emma's Bookstore Coffeehouse collective in Baltimore[3] (although somewhat different since we are entirely volunteers, and they are mostly able to pay themselves), there are different levels of expectations for those involved with the group. We bring new people along slowly; the soonest someone is able to be fully involved in the Shoe is six months. When people want to become part of the Wooden Shoe collective, they fill out an application. We then try to match up their schedules with the schedules of our trainers (staffers in the collective who have said that they are available to train new people).

The new applicants must do at least three trainings, which consist of showing them the ropes and helping them to become familiar with the politics and ins and outs of the collective. After completing their three trainings, they become a "new volunteer," a category that lasts for three months. The Wooden Shoe's expectations for volunteers are very loose, so people can find their way and decide how much they want to get involved. They are expected to staff only once a month, but can certainly staff more. They can choose to, but are not required to, be on any committees (such as the Finance Committee, Events Committee, Ordering Committees, or Conflict Mediation Committee). Likewise, they do not have to go to any meetings, but can if they so please. In our version of consensus decision-making, they cannot block any proposals from going forward.

Once three months have passed, a volunteer is eligible to receive keys and become a prospective member. Before explaining the nature of a "prospective member," I'll explain what a member does. Members are the collective core, built on mutual trust, regular communication, and committed work toward the collective. They have higher requirements, and thus are able to block proposals from going forward when it is time to make a decision. They are expected to go to half of the meetings (which are weekly). They should be involved in training new people in some manner. They should be on at least one committee.

The first meeting of the month is reserved specifically for members to talk about new trainees, the allocation of keys, prospective members, and accountability issues within the collective. The Wooden Shoe uses a quorum—half of the total number of members must be present for the collective to make decisions, and two-

The Wooden Shoe is based on anarchist principles of self-organization and collective decision-making. Despite widespread mischaracterization, anarchy is not about chaos and violence.

ANARCHY
is a type of ruling structure.

MONARCHY
is rule by a sovereign head of state, usually a king or queen.

OLIGARCHY
is rule by the wealthy elite.

PATRIARCHY
is rule by the father/male. And

ANARCHY
is rule by no one; there is no one ruler.

thirds of the total number of members must be present for members' meetings.

After three months, a volunteer can declare at any open meeting that s/he wishes to become a prospective member. At the following members' meeting, we decide whether to take the volunteer on as a prospective member (which we almost always do unless there are extreme circumstances). S/he then receives two sponsors from the membership—the prospective member might have asked sponsors in advance, or members can volunteer to sponsor someone. The role of the sponsors is to get the prospective member ready to become a member over the course of three months by training how to become a trainer, by getting her/him involved on a committee, and by making sure the prospective member is going to at least half the meetings. If all of these are completed over three months, then, at a members' meeting, we decide whether to make the person a member or not (again, we almost always accept prospective members who have completed the trainings unless there are extreme circumstances).

This system works quite well in making sure that the Shoe provides access for people who just want to plug in, as well as for people who want to jump totally into the organization, while at the same time giving older staffers a chance to slowly bring those folks along so they will be able to work in the group and for the long haul without burning themselves out. This organizational structure works well for a medium-sized group with 20 to 50 people involved, but, certainly, this is just one example of an organizational structure.

> We seek to be an example of the society we envision and it is that we are working towards as radicals. We are a non-profit space that works to offer ethical choices in what people buy, eat, drink, and learn. We are a non-hierarchical collective that hopes to empower members through worker self-management and a consensus decision-making process. As a collective, we are committed to discussing and challenging all systems of oppression, including but not limited to: racism, sexism, classism, heterosexism, ableism, and ageism within our own collective and in larger society. We seek to recognize

and identify various points of privilege we may have as members of a collective that is made up of people with unique identities, backgrounds, and histories. We hope to build a space that is part of a larger social movement that combines our resources with other cooperative and collective organizations locally and around the world for the purpose of mutual aid and the creation of a cooperative society.

— WOODEN SHOE STATEMENT OF VALUES, MARCH 2009

The Business Side of the Wooden Shoe

It is also important to recognize the business side of this operation. The Wooden Shoe operates as a business, even if it is a nonprofit, all-volunteer structure. This means we raise money by selling things. There is obviously a certain contradiction here, but we live and operate in a consumer, capitalist system. Since we live under the capitalist system, we use the tools of the master to agitate for the replacement of the master's system, to put it metaphorically. Unlike most groups, our fundraising consists of staying open by operating the bookstore. This means that all sold items are originally bought at a wholesale price. We then apply a standard markup of 40 percent, which basically goes toward (1) reordering books and other items, (2) upkeep of the space, and (3) paying the rent. We have a treasurer who is responsible for paying the bills and managing the bank account. In addition, we keep a daily sheet, which is filled out by each closer in order to keep track of the daily finances. This also enables us to catch staffers stealing money, which, fortunately, happens fairly rarely. In a nutshell: have a bank account, and rent a space in the standard way by signing a lease. It should be noted that, generally speaking, landlords don't care about your politics or what kind of space you are running as long as you pay the rent.

The Wooden Shoe operates to give people skills, to create a politically conscious community, and to provide a space for meeting people, talking about the world, and plugging into other groups, organizations, and causes. This kind of interaction is necessary for human sustenance and is a powerful tool for social change.

Minnesota United
for All Families: Vote No   (by Aaron Zellhoefer)

For years, US Representative Michelle Bachmann (R-MN) had been trying to make sure that LGBTQ individuals could never legally marry the people they love in Minnesota. She infamously prayed over the desk of Scott Dibble, an openly gay senator from Minnesota.

On election night 2010, the Tea Party, as a new radical faction of Republicans, won big in Minnesota. It was the first time in Minnesota history that the Republican Party had taken control of the Senate. Republicans now had control of both the House and the Senate. The only problem for them was that they did not have a Republican governor. The governor was Mark Dayton, representing the Democratic-Farmer-Labor (DFL) Party; he is still governor at the time of this writing. He has stood in the way of letting Republicans get what they want. The only way for Republicans to get around this is to put forward amendments to change the state constitution, and let the voters vote on it.

Wealthy business owner Robert Cummins has for years wanted a constitutional ban on gay marriage. Cummins has donated 3.3 million dollars to conservative causes since 1997. From 2004–2007, he gave 280,000 dollars to the Minnesota Citizens in Defense of Marriage federal fund. In 2005–2006, he handed over 128,130 dollars to Minnesota for Marriage; in 2006, the group spent 45,000 dollars to defeat then-Senate Majority Leader Dean Johnson, of the DFL Party. The attack ads against Johnson went after him for supporting a "radical homosexual agenda" and for blocking efforts to bring a constitutional amendment to ban same-sex marriage to the chamber floor. In 2012, Cummins and his wife Joan donated the maximum amount to Republican state Senator Warren Limmer.

Limmer was a chief author of a 2011 bill that sought to change the state constitution to clearly ban gay couples from ever getting married in Minnesota. Gay marriage was already illegal in the state; it had been that way since 1977, after a gay couple challenged for the right to get married. But on May 11, 2011, the Senate passed a bill allowing Minnesota voters to decide if they wanted to change the Minnesota constitution to limit marriage to only opposite-sex couples. The House passed a similar bill on May 21.

Enter Minnesota United for All Families, a group dedicated to opposing the amendment and encouraging voters to vote "no." The campaign was headed by Richard Carlbom,[4] a political communications specialist. The strategy was simple: have as many conversations with friends, family, and coworkers as possible. This campaign was unique in that it would not focus on specific rights that go along with marriage, such as tax breaks and hospital visitation rights, or on rights in general. Chants like "Gay, straight, black, white, marriage is a civil right" would not be used. Instead, this campaign would reframe the talking points from past campaigns, and focus on the core of marriage: love, commitment, responsibility, and support of the community. Those who were already married and were undecided on the amendment vote were asked about their own marriage, and asked why anyone should be denied that experience.

The idea of having conversations may seem too simplistic, but the social science literature on the subject is clear: *conversations in the context of friendship create change*. Telling stories in conversations is non-confrontational, and the person is more likely to listen to what you have to say, rather than get defensive and/or ignore your ideas. In brief, conversations invite people to consider your perspective and sympathize with your views and experiences.

After the state of Maine lost on a similar ballot question in 2010, a lot of research went into why supporters of same-sex marriage had lost. One important finding was that people who had LGBTQ friends and family members voted to limit the freedoms of LGBTQ individuals. But why? It was discovered that the LGBTQ persons they knew never told them how important winning against the ballot questions was to them. But when people *were* told by the LGBTQ individuals they knew, they were 67 percent more likely to vote in support of marriage equality.

To defeat the Minnesota ballot question, a lot of work needed to be done and a lot of conversations conducted. Polling was not on the side of LGBTQ individuals. A Survey USA poll in July 2012 found that 52 percent of Minnesotans would vote "yes" to change the constitution to deny LGBTQ couples the right to marry; 37 percent would vote "no" but allow the topic to be up for change at some point in the future; and five to six percent were still undecided.

Creating a Network of Activists

Minnesota United for All Families knew the challenge and organized the largest grassroots campaign the state had ever seen. The campaign was successful because it created a network of activists inside of an organizational structure.

- MUAF included 40,000 *volunteers* throughout the campaign, 28,000 of whom joined the campaign in the last week.
- Those volunteers had *conversations* all over the state, knocked on 400,000 doors the week before the election, and called 900,000 people the weekend before the election.
- MUAF comprised a *broad-based coalition* that included more than 700 organizations, including business, labor, nonprofits, governments, and faith-based organizations.
- MUAF included an *experienced staff* assembled from diverse political orientations (e.g., Democrats, Republicans, Greens, Independents).
- MUAF had a *communication team* that included social media and online media.
- MUAF had *lobbyists* working at the Minnesota capitol.

During an interview, Richard Carlbom was asked, "What advice would you give to other campaigns that are working either against such proposed legislation or in favor of marriage equality?" He responded:

1. *Start early.*
2. *Hire the best* staff, leaders, and organizers. Don't settle for second best.
3. Always, in all things you do, *deliver a research-driven message.* Research is essential to an effective message.
4. *Spark a conversation.*

Carlbom's advice has proven to work. On November 7, 2012, at 1:40 AM, the Associated Press called it a "no" vote. Carlbom took to the stage and announced to the nation that for the first time in US history, an anti-gay-marriage constitutional amendment had been defeated. "Tonight Minnesota proves that love is bigger than government," he said.

The final count was 1,399,916 "yes" votes and 1,510,434 "no" votes (40,430 did not vote on the question, and because of state law these votes were counted as "no" votes). A little more than 52 percent voted in support of same-sex marriage, which is consistent with national polls that show support for marriage equality at 53 percent.

At the time of this writing, the debate about marriage equality continues in the state of Minnesota. In February 2013, Governor Dayton said in his State of the State Address,

> Let me mention one other cause, which is controversial, but consistent with my faith and my principles and, more importantly, consistent with this country's founding principles and its Constitution. I believe that every Minnesotan should have the freedom to marry legally the person she or he loves, whether of the same or other sex. Last year, Minnesotans began a conversation about why marriage matters, and we found our common belief that it is about love, commitment, and responsibility. I want Minnesota to be a state which affirms that freedom for one means freedom for everyone, and where no one is told it is illegal to marry the person you love.[5]

Save the Kids   (by Anthony J Nocella II)

Save the Kids is a grassroots organization best summarized by its slogan—"a national movement to keep kids out of incarceration and away from violence." Its national headquarters is currently located in Saint Paul, Minnesota, and it has regional offices in Buffalo, Niagara, Syracuse, Chicago, Los Angeles, and Vermont. Save the Kids started in 2009 based on a conversation of four incarcerated youths about how community centers are not effective enough for the youth of the juvenile justice system. Those four youths at Hillbrook Youth Detention Facility in Syracuse, New York, created Save the Kids. At the time, I was a graduate student at Syracuse University and was a Life Skills teacher providing volunteer opportunities for college students to work with youth who were locked up. I helped those four youths start the organization.[6]

Hip-Hop Activism and Transformative Justice

Save the Kids, which was named by the original four kids, strives to be a national grassroots organization grounded in (1) hip-hop activism and politics; and (2) transformative justice. Indeed, non-corporatized hip-hop is one of the few efforts to educate youth of color in ways that move beyond the important though often reductive narratives of pre-slavery and colonialist histories.[7] Educational scholar Lance Williams emphasizes the potential power of this "counterhegemonic spirit of hip-hop such as narration of institutionalized racism, internal colonialism, underclass entrapment, and urban poverty"; such narratives "help explain the external sources of prevalent psychosocial problems among African American youth."[8] At its best, non-corporatized hip-hop is able to speak to the current conditions of poor urban communities, enabling and encouraging them to discuss, write, and rap about topics ranging from police brutality to the war on drugs.

The second emphasis of Save the Kids, transformative justice, goes beyond the classic victim-and-offender relationship and foregrounds the interrogation of systemic oppression. For instance, how might systems of racism, sexism, classism, or heteronormativity foster environments that motivate particular youth to make particular choices? And how do those choices then get those youth into legal troubles?

The U.S. **CONFINES** more of its **YOUTH** than any other country in the **WORLD.** As of 2010, there were approximately **70,790 YOUTH** (under the age of 21) **LOCKED UP** in various forms of youth detention facilities. This number does not include youth who are tried as adults. An additional **250,000 YOUTH UNDER AGE 18** are tried, sentenced, or incarcerated every year.

Transformative justice is rooted in community involvement and community accountability and emphasizes the end of punitive and retributive practices that include prisons, the death penalty, and torture.[9] Transformative justice tries to create community and government programs and services that are based on inclusive education, healing, forgiveness, and accountability by all those involved (e.g., offenders, victims, families, friends, police departments, laws, judges, the government).

Mission and Principles

The mission of Save the Kids is to advocate for alternatives to, and the end of, the incarceration of youths. Save the Kids has 10 principles:

1. We believe that all youth need support, love, and skills in order to achieve their goals.
2. We believe that all youth are amazing and wonderful no matter what actions they have committed.
3. We make a clear distinction between actions and kids; actions can be bad, but not kids.
4. We are committed to helping youth because they are our future, and if we do not help them, we will not have one.
5. We believe in respecting all, no matter their gender, ability, race, economic status, sexuality, religion, ethnicity, health, age, or nationality.
6. As a hip-hop activist organization, we work toward both social justice and the end of all forms of oppression and domination, specifically the school-to-prison pipeline.
7. As an organization based on transformative justice principles, we strive to promote alternatives to incarceration, such as community-based programs.
8. We believe in peace and nonviolence in resolving and transforming all conflicts.
9. We believe in not labeling, but rather in being inclusive in all of our activities.
10. We promote that everyone in the community should work together in making a peaceful world, not excluding anyone. Save

the Kids will work with everyone and anyone in order to achieve that goal.

The 3 BTWs

There are three basic methods for achieving the mission of Save the Kids. We refer to those methods as the 3 BTWs. The first is *Behind the Walls*, which is where Save the Kids began. This is a collaborative and experiential workshop facilitated by outside adults. Generally speaking, these workshops are facilitated on a weekly basis in youth detention facilities. The workshops cover life skills, politics, poetry, hip-hop, spoken word, job readiness, hygiene, conflict transformation, anger management, and social justice. This program allows outsiders to listen to the needs and wants of the youth who are locked up.

The second program, *Breaking The Walls*, involves street-style actions such as rallies, protests, candlelight vigils, sit-ins, speak-outs, days of silence, hunger fasts, pamphleteering, tabling, and boycotts. Topics that we cover include: stopping gun violence, understanding and ending America's rape culture, promoting community engagement in higher education, supporting incarcerated LGBTQ youth, dismantling the school-to-prison-pipeline, and challenging racism and poverty. Ideally, we will organize monthly events, with each regional chapter participating within its local community.

The third program is *Beyond the Walls*. This is more research-based, with scholars and experts writing articles, commentaries, and position papers, and reviewing pertinent books, films, or other media. The basic goal is to generate awareness and discussion about issues that relate to the incarceration of youth, hip-hop activism, and transformative justice.

Save the Kids is not a nonprofit organization with paid employees. Instead, it is a volunteer-based organization. We believe that if we are doing something good for people, then the people of the community will find ways to make it last and grow. We also believe that for a program to flourish, it must be run by those who are directly affected by the program's actions. In this case, we are talking about the families and friends of incarcerated youth and various community members who are interested in ending the criminal justice system. Save the Kids thus involves a broad coalition of professors, teachers, activists, community organizers, probation officers, social workers, school counselors, and former prisoners. The purpose is to help people come together and create positive change in their communities, both in the present moment and for future generations.

PART 4

SOCIAL NETWORKS

The Politics of Planning: Conference Organizing as an Act of Resistance

JENNY GRUBBS AND MICHAEL LOADENTHAL

But now with the living conditions deteriorating,
and with the sure knowledge that we are slated
for destruction, we have been transformed
into an implacable army of liberation.

— LETTER FROM GEORGE JACKSON
TO HIS LAWYER (APRIL 1970)

AS YOUNG ACTIVISTS, ACADEMICS, AND ACTIVIST-ACADEMICS, many of us spend far more weekends than we would like sitting in folding chairs listening to a presenter talk at us. A "convergence" provides a space to engage social justice aims, meet up with friends, create weekly to-do lists, or even knit a blanket for a child soon to be born. Some of us have attended these conferences, forums, seminars, and symposiums out of a sense of obligation and coercive pressure from our schools, employers, or communities. In some cases, we attend because we *want to*. These are the kinds of conferences we want to build.

This chapter is not about how to build stuffy, compulsory, talk-at-you-from-a-podium conferences. Rather, this guide walks you through the process of organizing liberatory gatherings that prefigure revolutionary change. In other words, we hope to facilitate the planning of public assemblies where we act in a manner that mirrors the world we want to see created.

We create conferences with free vegan food because we believe that no one should go hungry, and that justice cannot be achieved while we dine on the oppression of other beings. We create conferences with participation encouraged from all realms of society because we believe in a world of participatory democracy. We create conferences that encourage dialogue rather than diatribe, cooperation rather than coercion, and engagement rather than alienation.

It is incredibly important to continue the work of organizing. We must not only organize marches, demonstrations, and direct actions, but we must also create physical spaces where we leave the message boards, comment streams, and blogs behind and meet one another as allies. It is only through these face-to-face encounters that some things may be accomplished.

FACE-TO-FACE interactions build trust, friendship, and shared experience. These are **ESSENTIAL** for activism, organizing, and social movements.

Through meeting one another, we can build networks of trust, collectively engage in mutual aid projects, and share stories and experiences. In corners tucked away during lunch breaks, we can conspire and plot our attacks against the evils of this world. Over a cup of tea, waiting for the first panel to begin, we can share newfound ways of making change. In some cases, these chance meetings may even blossom into lifelong partnerships, with individuals finding commonalities in struggle, in education, or in friendship.

What follows in this chapter is an exploration of conference organizing as a foundational aspect of activism and education. This chapter was collaboratively written by two people and is the product of a series of conversations addressing these core questions. We have traveled across the North American continent together presenting, attending, *and* organizing, and it is from these experiences that we write this guide. We write collaboratively as an act of resistance, and as an example of transparency, exposing the hidden skill set learned through trial and error. This guide was produced with the belief that collaboration is essential to enacting social change.

Activist Separatists:
Why Activists Should Organize and Meet

Just as the Black Panthers sought to organize among their own community, sometimes as activists it just makes sense for us to make our own space. The National Conference on Organized Resistance (NCOR), held annually in Washington, DC, from 1998–2008, is a good example of an activist conference. NCOR was attended by well over a thousand activists annually and served a number of key functions in our movements, particularly the rise in counter-summit organizing that took off following the 1999 World Trade Organization protests in Seattle. Other activist conferences include Finding Our Roots (Chicago), All Power to the Imagination (Sarasota), the BASTARD Conference (Berkeley), and anarchist book fairs in cities throughout the US.

TAZ
Temporary Autonomous Zone

So why should activists organize such conferences? Let's explore some of the reasons below:

- We can *create temporary spaces* to experiment with alternative methods of horizontal organization. We are able to conduct experiments in organizing free child care; distributing large-scale food, not bombs; negotiating the politics of non-gendered bathrooms, and even a bit of urban exploring to find places for traveling attendees to catch some sleep. We can create what Hakim Bey calls "Temporary Autonomous Zones," where we can explore new, prefigurative ways of mutual aid and solidarity. We can even use these TAZs to distribute zines, plan national campaigns, coordinate marches, plot revolution....
- We can cross-pollinate movements. For example, an activist trainer with the Ruckus Society may teach a room full of activists how to conduct a well-executed banner drop, videotape an action, or build a better barricade. These skills can be learned on

site and then taken back to home communities by the attendees
and used in campaigns all around the world. At NCOR, we saw
the Radical Cheerleaders of DC teach radical cheerleading, the
Down There Health Collective teach do-it-yourself sexual health,
and we even saw Rod Coronado teach a room full of activists how
to build a milk jug incendiary device.

- We can distribute financial (mutual) aid. The George Jackson
  Brigade called it "expropriating the expropriators," but we call it
  solidarity. For example, a conference held at a university (with the
  school subsidizing some of the costs) may be given a budget that
  can help send money downwards—from large funding institutions to individual activists and activist projects.

- We can allow direct-action movements to recruit activists, and
  folks who are already active in these struggles to network. This
  is a great way for individuals to get linked up to national and international campaigns seeking participants and co-conspirators.
  Campaigns such as Stop Huntingdon Animal Cruelty, the International Solidarity Movement, Earth First!, Bash Back!, and the
  Sea Shepherd Conservation Society regularly hosted workshops
  at NCOR and were able to grow their ranks through direct outreach.

- We can provide a semi-safe space for illegal direct-action movements to grow. While it would be foolish to distribute copies of
  The Animal Liberation Front Primer at an activist conference, it is
  not uncommon to find an unattended table covered in copies of
  tactical guides and other materials. All you need is an area to set
  up and a single piece of paper that says, "FREE take as many as
  you'd like!" This is how we first saw guides such as *Delia Smith's
  Basic Blockading* or *Bodyhammer: Tactics and Self-Defense for the
  Modern Protester.*

- We can provide a site to disseminate our movements' publications. You can bring a small box of your group's latest magazines
  or DVD and send people back to their respective regions with
  materials to disperse. This was done widely with DIY publica-

tions such as CrimethInc's *Fighting for Our Lives* and early issues of magazines such as *Bite Back*, *Left Turn*, *off our backs*, and *Green Anarchy*.

- We can come together and carry out an action with the presence of tons of activists in one city at the same time. For example, NCOR attendees often joined local anti-fur protests at Neiman Marcus, and some nightly concerts became jumping-off points for anti-capitalist marches through wealthy commercial districts.
- We can meet other activists. Through organizing regional caucuses, we can meet activists in our area. Through queer/women/youth/people of color caucuses, we can get support from others facing similar struggles.

These are just *some* of the many reasons it is important for activists to have their own conferences. Here we can have the time, space, and freedom to become better, more well-connected peacemakers, revolutionaries, and clandestine agents for total insurrection.

A Guide to Conference Organizing

The following guidelines can (and should) be utilized as an organizing tool. Each convergence is unique, and we all make executive decisions as members within a collective. The guide is meant to facilitate the uniqueness of your event, and help you actualize the aspirations and goals into a tangible event for the community. Our radical spaces exist within the intersections of people's lives, and we must remain conscious of our community. With each step of the process, you should always consider issues of inclusion and physical accessibility—breastfeeding, public transportation, on-site child care, community-hosted housing, gender-neutral bathrooms, local and fair-trade commodities used in food and beverages provided, and the list goes on. Our events must be examples of the change we wish to see in the world. These guidelines are by no means exhaustive, but they do represent our experiences of organizing both activist and academic conferences throughout the years.

Grand Planning

1. **Decide your budget:** Will you charge a fee to attend the conference? Do you have sources of funding from schools, community groups, NGOs, individual sponsors? Examine your budget, your costs for the space, and make decisions as to what you can and cannot provide. Will your conference serve food? Food is political, so carefully decide what types of food (local? vegan? seasonal? purchased or freecycled?). Will the conference provide child care? What about funding assistance for attendees and presenters? Will you help find people a place to stay? Will you help people with transportation? Will you be hosting nighttime entertainment? All of these decisions will likely be based on how much money you are able to raise. If you expect 200 attendees, and calculate that you would need three to four thousand dollars to organize a conference, charging people a sliding-scale attendance fee of 15 to 20 dollars would work just fine and would be within reach for most people.

2. **Locate a physical space that meets your needs:** Make sure you consider cost, space, and accessibility. Some conferences will require one or two large rooms, while others will need several smaller rooms. Some require audiovisual capacity for showing films and computer presentations, and others require that participants and presenters be able to sit in a circle. Typical sites for large conferences are universities, religious spaces, community centers, cultural centers, labor halls, and hotels. Most likely, your biggest challenge will be finding a space large enough and within your budget. Each type of space has its own positives and negatives. University spaces can often be utilized for free if the conference is organized as part of an on-campus club, but may restrict services such as food, housing, and child care due to stringent university-wide liability/insurance issues. Religious spaces such as large churches may allow folks to sleep and cook on-site, but may be alienating to secular and other attendees. Hotels may have state-of-the-art presentation equipment and comfort perks such as a

pool, restaurant, or gym, but may be overly costly. Community and cultural centers may be familiar spaces to your community and provide attendees with a bit of comfort and familiarity, but may have less availability and less ability to provide assistance (e.g., security, housekeeping, food service). Try to brainstorm issues specific to your community that will help ensure that your attendees feel comfortable and safe. For example, what will the bathroom situation be like in a given facility? Will it have gender-neutral restrooms?

3. **Choose a date:** Consider how far in advance people may need to know about the conference in order to attend. Consider the cost of travel at different times of the year. Consider the weather. Think of all the different people you may want to attend and the challenges they face. Try to pick a date that works *for the most people possible.* No date will work for everyone, so don't get discouraged. Depending on how many people are attending and how far they are traveling, pick a date far enough in the future. For a conference with more than a few hundred people, try to pick a date *at least* six months in advance.

Outreach and Organizing the Particulars

1. **Identify who you would want to attend:** What is your constituency? Is this a conference for activists, academics, students, volunteers, community members, professionals, employees? Is this a conference for anarchist activists, transgendered youths, service-industry workers, future teachers, radical anthropologists, students and academics concerned with the criminalization of dissent, organizers planning events to coincide with a specific mobilization?

2. **Begin to map out where your potential attendees are located** and make a distribution list to help with outreach to the folks you want to attend. This can be done based on location (the New York area), a shared topic of interest (queer insurrection), a shared politic (post-left anarchism), and so on. This initial list should

be based around the conference you *hope* to create, not simply the distance between the events and those invited. Contact those you identify via whatever means are most effective (e.g., email, phone, postal service, online social networks), and tell them your plans for a conference. Tell them the location and the date. Ask if they can help you circulate your formal announcement for participants when it is ready in the coming weeks.

3. **Mobilize committees** to handle various aspects of the conference. It takes several smaller (sub)committees to handle the logistics: committees for scheduling, housing, food (can be two committees: food prep and food serving), keynote search, technology, and feedback. You also want to start recruiting people to form necessary committees for the actual conference event. This includes registration desk, tabling, food serving, technology (ranging from audiovisual hookup to microphone issues to taking photographs throughout the event), and cleanup. Identify a core group of people who can be publicly identified within the conference body as organizers. These people will answer questions, direct people, and address concerns of attendees on the spot. Organizing a conference within a collective requires patience, dedication, empathy, and a whole lot of extra time, so try and ensure that folks agree to take on only tasks they can handle. "Many hands make light work."

4. **Develop a "call" for presenters:** While the main focus of the announcement is to sure up initial presenters and workshop leaders, a widely circulated call can also help promote the event for attendees, and gather feedback for future outreach. Sometimes this announcement will take the form of a formal Call for Papers (CFP). Sometimes it will be a more informal announcement that says, "Hey, we're having a conference about this topic, and we would love to hear from you if you're interested in participating." This "call" will be as formal or as informal as your venue and conference require. Make sure the announcement contains as much important logistical information as possible, including the six key questions:

Who:

- Who is organizing the conference?
- Who is invited to attend?
- Will you have a keynote speaker(s)?

What:

- What is the conference about and why?
- Is there a theme?
- What is being offered in terms of services (e.g., food, housing, transportation, funding, child care, opportunities to present, opportunities to volunteer)?

When:

- What is the date or approximate date of the conference?
- Is it one day or multiple days?
- Is it full day(s) or half-day(s)? Only at night?

Where:

- Is the conference at a hotel, university, squat…?
- Is it indoors, or at a campsite?
- Will the location have housing?
- Is it easily accessible by popular forms of transportation (e.g., airport, train station, bus line)?

Why:

- What is the purpose of the gathering?
- Why is it important?

How:

- What are the deadlines? When are proposals due? When will presenters be notified?
- Where can people write or call for more information or questions? Is there a website, blog, or other place to look for updates as they develop?

This "call" should contain all of the information above and more as you see fit. It should also be as short as possible. Since this is the first announcement you are sending out to a wide audience, it should be clear and to the point. It should convey as much information as possible and also *tell people what you are asking them to do.* Are you asking people to send you workshop proposals, paper abstracts, ideas for panels? Are you asking people to RSVP and let you know how many are attending? Are you asking people to let you know if they are interested so that you can contact them directly and speak to them one-on-one? Make sure the expectations and deadline are clear, for example, "Please send workshop descriptions—including a title, 300–500-word description, and brief presenter biography—to us at conferenceorganizers@conference.com by January 1, 2013. We will get back to you by January 20 to let you know if your workshop has been accepted." The next page shows an example of a simple call for an activist conference

1. **Blast your "call"** to the folks you want to attend. Make sure to vary the form in which this is done. No one technique will ever reach a wide and diverse group. Utilize direct emails, email listservs, social networking sites such as Facebook/Twitter, printed flyers, announcements at other events, posters in key places such as infoshops/cafes/radical spaces, phone calls, sidewalk chalk, etc. Post your announcement on sympathetic websites, forums, blogs, and news service sites. Figure out where your desired audience goes to learn about these events.

2. **Develop a set of criteria to evaluate presentations.** How will you decide which to include and which to exclude? Who gets to decide? Is there a vote? Do you use consensus? Set aside a period to review the proposed presentations, allowing enough time for concerns to be raised and questions to be asked. Discuss the presentations and decide which ones you would like to include. Envision the schedule before making final decisions. You need physical space and time for each presentation, so it is important you do not accept more proposals than can be accommodated.

3. **Contact *all* the people who submitted proposals** and let them know what was decided. Thank those you have accepted, and

———— **PLEASE FORWARD WIDELY** ————

National Conference on Revolutionary Squirrel Watching
May 1–3, 2013
Old Town Labor Hall
555 Main Street, Anytown, PA 12345

Call for Proposals: Workshops, films, round-table discussions The National Conference on Revolutionary Squirrel Watching (NCRSW) is an annual event bringing together squirrel enthusiasts from a range of backgrounds for a weekend of learning, organizing, and networking.

We are currently seeking workshop, film, and round-table discussion proposals for the 22nd annual NCRSW conference, after last year's successful gathering. In 2013, NCRSW XXI saw over 100 workshops, films, and discussions, and well over 2,000 attendees! We welcome any and all small-animal enthusiasts to attend this year as well, to make 2014 the year of the squirrel!

Please send our organizers your 1- to 2-page proposals. Make sure you include (1) your name, the organization you are representing (if applicable), contact information, and a short biography about you and/or your organization; (2) the title of your workshop, film, or round-table; (3) whether you would like a one-, two-, or three-hour time slot; and (4) the format of your presentation. Please send these proposals to blacksquirrel@iheartsquirrels.com by January 1, 2014. We will contact all presenters by January 20, 2014, to let you know if your proposal has been accepted.

For more information, outreach materials, and a forthcoming schedule, visit our blog at blogsite.com.

———— **PLEASE FORWARD WIDELY** ————

thank those you have decided not to accept, as well. Invite those you did not accept to attend anyway. Set a deadline for presenters to confirm their participation, specifically asking if they have any time or travel constraints that should be considered during the planning process.

4. **Make a schedule grid** once the confirmation deadline has passed, and place presenters in time slots. This can take a great deal of time, and works best with a committee. Some presentations may have to overlap. Some presenters can travel or attend only on certain days or at certain times. If you are trying to decide which panels to overlap, make sure those addressing similar themes do not overlap, preventing someone with a particular topical interest from following a consistent "course of study." If you have a plenary or keynote, pencil that in first. Once you have created a tentative schedule, draw up a draft. This could be as simple as:

Schedule: Confronting Sexual Assault in Radical Communities 2014

TIME	NAME	FORMAT	TITLE	LOCATION
10–11 am	Amanda Huginkis	Film	No Means No!	Victory Hall, room 221
11 am–1 pm	Noah Fence	Workshop	Understanding Consent	Johnson Center, basement conference room
LUNCH 1:30–2:30, Main Dining Hall				
3–5 pm	Rhoda Byke	Discussion	Being an Ally	Center for Justice, room 2
5–7 pm	Justin Kase	Activity	Yoga for Trauma Healing	West courtyard lawn, under the old oak tree
CLOSING PANEL: "The Future of Solidarity Against Assault," Main Lecture Hall (2nd floor) 8–9pm				

Send the schedule to presenters for final review. How open to changes will you be? If you are able to modify the schedule, send it to participants for review with a clear deadline to respond. If you are not able to modify the schedule and someone expresses a preference for a different time than shown on the schedule, you can state that accommodation requests were due by an earlier date and are no longer able to be considered.

1. **Publicize the schedule** through all of the sources you used to send out the "call." Utilize social networking, both in person and through technology. Do you have any connections to print outlets? College campuses maintain listservs in each department and will often send out announcements; contact the administrative assistant in the department and request that the announcement be released. Create a Facebook event page, a free website on a blog (like wordpress.com or blogspot.com), and seek out event-listing pages.

2. **Make sure all of the committees (and subcommittees) schedule final, pre-event meetings.** It will be up to these groups to determine what is still left to do and to decide how those tasks are divided. These meetings should be scheduled for at least a week in advance of the conference to go over all the details.

Day of the Conference

1. **Check in with the committees:** Make sure each committee has the resources and support necessary to take care of its responsibilities during the conference without being micromanaged. Empowerment is essential. The food committee should report on its budget and plans to serve food. Ask if they need any extra hands or transportation requests to bring the food to the conference site. Do they have enough people to help serve and clean up? Ask the scheduling committee if there are any last-minute changes (cancellations or technology requests). Does the technology committee have any questions about audiovisuals; does it have a name and number for someone affiliated with the conference site in case last-minute issues arise with electricity or computers? Do you have enough people to sit at the registration desk? Are there any times that need to be covered? Does the merchandise committee need extra space for tablers?

2. Someone from the **registration committee** will need to get to the conference site at least 30 minutes prior to the start of registration time. The committee will assemble name tags and set out a

box to collect fees (e.g., registration or food), if applicable. The first shift of registration desk volunteers will help direct newly arriving participants to the presentation rooms and refreshments, and complete their check-in. Also during this time, if the event is hosting tables for vendors and/or organizations to distribute/ sell materials, someone from the organizing committee should be on site to help set this up before the majority of attendees arrive. Since most tablers will arrive with the morning attendee rush, it is good for this set-up to occur during early-morning registration so as to not overwhelm people staffing registration.

3. The **food committee** should be at the site early to set up water, coffee and tea (if available) and any other provided edibles. If things need to be refrigerated for later meals, unpack these items and store them as early as possible. Get the kitchen prepared for the entire day—it might be too hectic later to do so. Hot water and coffee urns take about 20 minutes to prep, so make sure that time is allotted. If you are serving food, keep in mind (1) oven preheating, (2) whether you will have access to water in the kitchen area, and (3) where people will be able to eat (tables? chairs? couches? on the floor?). Make sure the space is accessible (e.g., do not serve food upstairs if the building does not have an elevator). Have a plan for what you will do with excess food. Will you donate? How will it get there?

4. **Technology committee members** should briefly visit each room during the presentations. Make sure presenters have a phone number for a member of the technology committee who they can contact from the presentation room in case of emergency.

5. If you are **providing child care**, have the committee's contact person distribute a phone number to allow parents leaving kids to check in. Also, make sure those providing the child care have at least two phone numbers for parents in case they need to be contacted with a question or in the event of an emergency. Emergencies can arise, and people may need assistance at the last minute. Will you have a space for breastfeeding? What about for napping? If so, make sure that information is widely available.

6. **Double-check accessibility concerns.** Make sure ramps are in place, elevators (if applicable) are operating properly, translators are present, and any other accessibility concerns addressed. What is the bathroom situation like in the facility? Is it necessary to hang event-specific signs—for example, to change "Men's" and "Women's" restroom signs to read "Gender Neutral"?

7. **Those identified to be key contact persons** during the conference should walk around often. Make sure panels are running on time. Wear some identifiable tag or shirt so that attendees know they can approach you. Touch base with the committees and make sure they do not need anything.

8. **After the main event is over, but before attendees leave the site,** mobilize the feedback committee to distribute surveys or questionnaires, or to facilitate discussion groups. Whatever the method, make sure participants have a space to voice their praise and constructive criticism to the organizers; it will help for planning next year.

9. **Although everyone should pitch in for the cleanup effort,** this is when the cleanup committee comes in handy. Divide tasks—folding chairs and tables, emptying trash, removing signs, cleaning up litter, making sure the restrooms are not trashed, checking the fridge and kitchen area for any leftover items. Make sure the space is left in the same condition it was found in, if not cleaner.

10. **Schedule a meeting within one week after the conference** to discuss how the event unfolded. Make sure committee members are represented and heard. Go over the participant feedback collected from the conference. If you intend to run the conference again, generate a list of those interested in volunteering.

Washington, DC (2002):
A Vignette of Two Conference-Goers

Conferences are where we get out from behind our computers, our books, our fundraising drives, and our petitions and meet one another to share, conspire, and learn. It is where we build our communities and where we grow our ideas.

At one particular conference, held in the North American mid-Atlantic, two community organizers started up a conversation after they found themselves both excitedly reading the same book jacket— Dave Foreman's *Ecodefense: A Field Guide to Monkeywrenching*. The two were from small towns over 700 miles away, but on this occasion, their shared passion for the wondrous beauty of nature brought them together. Once they noticed their connection, it was out of their hands. This was the type of connection that no blog, online forum, or Indymedia comment thread could emulate. Neither one of them had much money, so they decided to purchase one copy of the book and read it together. They each put in their five dollars, picked up the book, and quickly went off to a corner to gobble up its contents. They skipped all the workshops that day. The two of them read that book from cover to cover by the end of the day.

That next day they woke up extra early and met again at the conference, this time with their backpacks. They went to the opening panel, said goodbye to their travel buddies, friends, and colleagues, and started off for the bus station. They left together. A few weeks later, news reports began to announce that a series of actions seemed to be marking a trail west. First there was an animal liberation near Lexington, Kentucky, followed by some tree spikings in southwestern Missouri. Then reports surfaced about actions in Boulder, Salt Lake City, Boise, and Eugene. The police indicated that at each site a small note was left that read, "Hearts united burning free, defending the Earth from the sea to the sea." While no one was ever arrested for these acts, I'd like to think that some who attended that conference and might have seen those two smirking in the corner may well have their own theories....

Final Thoughts

No guide can fully cover every basis, every contingency, and every possible pitfall. At the first conference that we attended, there was a sexual assault at the conference's nighttime social event. The conference organizers decided that the closing plenary that was to occur the following day would be replaced by a group workshop that dealt with sexual assault in activist communities. This ad hoc crisis response planning was an attempt to integrate radical praxis into the methods of conflict resolution, and a prime example of the unpredictability involved in conference organizing. The specifics of that particular event are irrelevant, but it was important that the conference organizers did not let the incident remove the focus on prefigurative, egalitarian social change. The methods of conflict resolution attempted to reflect the politics of the space and the views of the attendees. The session did not "fix" the issue of sexual assault in activist communities; however, it did demonstrate that the organizers were committed to the political nature of the project at hand.

Organizing a conference is a political act. Each decision is made with intention, has multiple implications, and influences a wide audience of peoples. From those who attend, to those who feel excluded and refuse to attend, to those whom you continuously reach out to and *eventually* convince to attend, these spaces have the potential to be anti-exclusionary, and, at best, they dare to be transgressive. Each event provides a space for dialogue and an opportunity to create community. As long as we keep this central to our planning, we can continue to build for a better world and to let our methods mirror the world we want to create instead of replicate the world we want to change. This guide reflects our struggles, triumphs, and optimism for the future. We learn from our mistakes as organizers, and remain hopeful that we will do better next time.

8

Social Media and Online Organizing

JEANETTE RUSSELL[1]

*Technology has unlocked the doors and facilitated
a genuine democratization of our culture. No longer
content to sit on the sidelines as spectators,
a new generation of participants is taking
an active role in our culture and democracy.*

—MARKOS MOULITSAS ZUNIGA

THIS CHAPTER PROVIDES GUIDELINES FOR USING SOCIAL media for social change. The first section provides a brief overview of how social media impacts the contemporary world. The second section outlines some of the basic tools of social media—websites, email, Facebook, Twitter, Google, etc. The third section applies some basic organizing principles to the use of social media—targeting powerbrokers, shaping your message, developing social media content, and so on. The fourth section discusses strategies for expanding your activist network via social media. The fifth and final section provides a real-life example of how one activist, John Hlinko of Left Action, expanded his activist network to over 1,000,000 progressives through the strategic use of social media.

The Social Revolution

It is obvious that our contemporary lives are technologically inter-connected. But this was not always the case. Having the choice to plug into a human network at a moment's notice is nothing short of a social revolution. And that social revolution has influenced the world of activism and organizing.

Activism is no longer limited to traditional nonprofits or traditional forms of organizing. Everyone is now a potential activist. Facebook, Twitter, LinkedIn, YouTube, and even basic websites and emails are tools of activism. People are quickly learning how to use these technologies to organize around issues of transparency, democracy, and far-reaching social change. People everywhere are combining online and offline organizing tactics like never before to pressure companies, elected officials, and even brutal dictatorships to listen and change—or be undermined, boycotted, and even over-thrown.

Broadband, mobile connectivity, and Internet accessibility are major reasons why it's easier for folks to organize quickly and successfully. On the one hand, these technologies affect (and are an effect of) consumerism—i.e., products are designed, manufactured, sold, and bought with an eye toward techno-connectivity. People want their phones, websites, TVs, email, and games connected to the people and things that they care about. Increasingly, products are designed with sharing integration in mind, which helps drive the seamless connectivity for more people to join the daily conversation.

On the other hand, such connectivity influences how people *solve social and political problems.* Groups of people are able to quickly analyze problems and come up with better solutions because they are forced to look at many points of view and utilize collective wisdom. This model of collective intelligence has been a huge part of social movements for well over a decade: e.g., in the Global Justice movement of the late 1990s–early 2000s, the Anti-Iraq War movement of the early/mid-2000s, the Arab Spring, and the Occupy movement.

If you think all of this technology is hard to keep up with because it changes so fast, you're correct. *Digital change is exponential.* It's generally believed that computing capacity doubles every few years, which is one of the reasons why social technologies move so quickly. In 2011, 65 percent of online adults in the US used social media sites such as Facebook, Twitter, and LinkedIn.[2] Given the trend of increasing social media use, it's reasonable to think that this number might be close to 100 percent in the near future; and given how quickly technology advances, it's reasonable to think that social media will look completely different than it does now.

Between the time I write this and the time this book is published, computing capacity will increase, new tools will come and go, and the specific how-tos of social networking may be outdated. I therefore believe that the how-tos of individual tools are less important than having a solid understanding of the strategies for using them (i.e., the actual organizing through social media). After all, if it were as easy as posting your actions to Facebook, we'd have world peace by now.

While this chapter is focused on social media, it's really about how to use communication technologies in a more general sense. People might refer to this general subject as social media, new media, online organizing, or social networking. Theses labels will change and evolve as quickly as our technology, so what we call it is not that important. Understanding how these online tactics fit into your larger strategy for change is the key.

Outlining the Basic Tools

Below are some tips on how to use the most popular social media tools. Some are basic; some are more advanced. But all of them are important for social change. This section should give you a quick overview of what is out there (and what many of you might already know).

Websites

Your website is one of your primary tools. It's where people learn more about your movement, cause, event, and/or organization. It should be relevant to your target audience, easy to find and navigate, and shareable. This is your public face, so it had better be good, especially for repeat visitors. Ask yourself, why would people want to visit your site? Is it for the content, to build and participate in community, to stay updated on current affairs?

- **User experience:** A question you should ask yourself when designing your site is, "What do I want folks to do?" Also consider how social you want your website to be. Do you want to encourage dialogue and collaboration, build followers, promote community, engage with actions? The site should be mapped with this in mind. If you want someone to take action on important issues, this should be front and center on your homepage. Many groups find success posting the latest news on the homepage with a call to action.

- **Capture contacts:** If you are an organization that wants to continually expand your network, then it's essential that your site capture contact information of potential supporters. You absolutely need to get the contact information of visitors if you ever want to organize them. Prioritize capturing their emails, first names, and zip codes, so you know where they live, allowing you to build neighborhood, city, and/or regional coalitions. The most common way to get contact information is via web forms that allow people to sign up for enews, sign petitions, donate, sign up for events, and/or volunteer. Contributing contact information should be easy for the user and, ideally, it should automatically go into your "Constituent Relational Management" system when forms are filled out and submitted. (A CRM is basically a database.)

- **Content management system (CMS):** If you are an organization with goals of expanding, then you need to think about your site's content management system. Your CMS should allow you to easily make updates to your site's content. There are free CMS tools such as WordPress that have a ton of built-in basic web templates and that are user friendly. At some point, you might consider paying for customization and design, and for annual updates. (If you know someone who can do such work for free, then great. But realize that professional quality is a lot of work that can cost some money.)

- **Integrate social media:** I will discuss specific social media just below, but in reference to websites, you want to make it easy for supporters, followers, friends, and fellow activists to (1) share and comment on content; and (2) feel a sense of involvement and participation—this builds community and strengthens coalitions. Include a one-click ability for folks to re-post to the most popular sites such as Facebook, Twitter, and Google+. Things that are often shared include blog posts, news, events, calls to action, updates, videos, and announcements about donating funds to your campaign or organization.

Email

- **Email is still the killer app:** Email may seem old and boring, but it is still one of the best ways to communicate. It's not explicitly social because it's designed for one-way communication to a specific person or group of people. The social component enters when you let your network of activists and organizers share your emails through icons and tell-a-friend forms in the email that allow folks to post to social network sites (e.g., Facebook and Twitter). Keep in mind that your email audience will probably be different from your blog, Facebook, or Twitter audience—your emails will probably be slightly more personal than a Twitter post, for instance, and they can be slightly longer, too.

- **Email metrics:** This is much more advanced and probably not needed if you are organizing a single protest or action. But if you are a nonprofit organization with hopes of longevity, then this is something to look into. In general, email metrics allow you to assess and keep track of your base supporters. You'll want to understand the open, click-through, conversion, and unsubscribe rates. The conversion rate is the most important metric, since it tells you how many people actually did what you asked. For example, if you sent a petition to five thousand people and five hundred took action, you'd have an impressive 10 percent conversion rate. While there are limits to what such metrics can tell you, it's important to know your baseline so you can evaluate the general effectiveness of an email. Doing a quick online search for "email metrics" will give you plenty of sites and sources to self-educate.
- **Email arc:** You know you're becoming an effective social media activist when you can effectively map out a smart "email arc." An email arc is basically a short story that addresses three things: why the email recipient should participate and get involved; why s/he should act *now*; and what s/he should actually do. An email arc is often sent in a series of three emails that tells a story. Also, since the average conversion rate for an advocacy email is about 10 percent (and only .05 percent on fundraising emails), you'll get more mileage by repurposing the email and sending it three times. Here's an example of a great email arc by Moms Rising, an organization that fights for family issues. Its goal at the time was to organize its members to lobby for healthcare.
  - Email 1: We're coming to a city near you!
  - Email 2: Can you join us at a local US Senate meeting to talk about healthcare?
  - Email 3: We're going to the US Capitol today—back us up online!
- **Mobile email:** Today, it is fairly common to read emails through our phones. Keep this in mind when you design your email. How will your banner, photos, text, buttons, and text placement look on a phone? The design has a significant impact on the success of any call to action.

Other Social Media Tools

- **Facebook:** For better or for worse, Facebook is part of many people's everyday lives, thus making it a great tool for activism. In general, people love videos and photos. You can also post questions with the hope that people will respond and start conversations. Realize, too, that the large majority of the people who see your updates will see them through their Facebook newsfeed, not on your Facebook page—therefore, keep it short and sweet. Also think about Facebook vs. your own separate website. Many people are foregoing websites and simply using Facebook. This saves money and time. But your own website can look more professional and leave a more lasting impression. If possible, do both.

- **Twitter:** Twitter is an online social networking and microblogging service that enables users to send and receive "tweets"—short text messages limited to 140 characters. Contrary to what one might think, Twitter should not be used as a megaphone to blast out announcements. Instead, use it as a platform for conversation. In other words, don't make it all about you—retweet liberally and highlight what others are doing in your sector, movement, or coalition. Run campaigns, sure, but also have fun and be human and authentic. Here's a 60-30-10 rule: 60 percent of your tweets should offer value by pointing to others' tweets or resources; 30 percent should be about responding and connecting with others; and 10 percent should be self-promotional or making announcements.

- **Google+:** Google+ (pronounced *Google plus*) is an online social networking service that lets users post messages and status updates like Twitter and Facebook, but also allows for other social actions, such as video chats and posting photos. Don't overlook the potential impact of Google+. If you've used it and haven't gotten far in spurring conversation threads, it's still valuable to use it for one reason: your posts to Google+ will turn up in some people's Google search results.

- **YouTube:** We all know YouTube is a great tool. How many videos do we watch on a regular basis? How many conversations have we had about the latest YouTube phenomenon? Posting raw footage—from street actions, mass arrests, or even speaker events—can get you attention. But it is also a good idea to take some time to create an original video. The actual content can be raw street footage or it can be purposefully shot. Either way, you should think like a movie director. What do the shots, sounds, and camera angles communicate to people? Do I need to edit and craft this? What message is it sending to my audience?

- **Google and YouTube:** If you're a 501(c)(3), make sure you take 15 minutes and apply to be part of Google for Nonprofits,[3] which gets you access to YouTube for Nonprofits, Google Grants for Nonprofits, and much more. Use YouTube to tell your organization's story, although you'll probably want to embed the video on your own site rather than spend a lot of effort trying to foster conversations on YouTube itself.

- **LinkedIn:** Whereas Facebook is used mostly for social networking, LinkedIn is used mostly for professional networking. If you use LinkedIn—whether as an individual or as an organization— make sure you keep your information updated. Spell out your cause or mission, and sync up some of your other social media accounts so people can see your latest tweets and posts right from LinkedIn.

The Latest App Might Die, but Organizing Principles Stand the Test of Time

The above tools are obviously important. But realize that all the tools in the world won't help you reach your social and political goals if you do not have an effective plan of action. You should thus think of yourself as an organizer rather than as a social mediaist. Are the two related and can they be combined? Yes and yes. But the former comes before the latter. To put it another way, social media is *not* the end. Your social and political goals are the end; social media helps you achieve those ends. To be a successful organizer, you must clearly understand goals, target audiences, and strategies. Then, after all of that work is done, you begin to implement particular social media. Below are some key principles to consider when developing this kind of approach.

- **Define your goal:** What is your main purpose? What is your rallying cause? What are you trying to accomplish? It could be something as grand as passing anti-nuclear legislation or as simple as erecting a peace sign in your community. Your goal should also answer "Why now?" so it makes sense to a broad audience who will be more likely to participate. Most importantly, your goal should be achievable with clear benchmarks to show progress. People want to be part of a winning team. You'll need to show continual momentum so you have enough people power to cross the finish line. Most campaigns have a short window to leverage their power. Create a plan that identifies your goals, strategies, and tactics with a few timelines in mind. Generally, the longer it takes you to reach your goal, the more challenging it will be to maintain your people power.

The tools of **SOCIAL MEDIA** are effective only if you know how to be a **POLITICAL ORGANIZER.**

- **Designate the powerbrokers:** If you are trying to influence policy, whether at the highest national or international level or the lowest local level, there are a handful of people who have the power to make it happen. Find out who they are—*these* are the folks you need to influence. A good target also needs to be transferable—if a member of Congress won't listen to you, then perhaps his or her campaign donors will. Following the money is a great way to get someone's attention—donors, advertisers, and investors who fund projects and candidates are very interested in how their money is being spent and whether or not politicians are passing the kind of policies that the politicians promised during their campaigns.

- **Strive for people power:** Since you probably don't have enough money to really influence the political machine (which is the case for most peace and justice activists), you will need people power and lots of it. This means you need a plan for how to recruit new supporters and how to effectively engage them. This is everything for an organizer. Without a strong supporter base, you will have a very difficult time getting anywhere. But that's not the case with a thousand people. And think how much power you have with fifty

or a hundred thousand people. Imagine having enough supporters to equal a small town—now *that's* people power!

- **Understand your issue:** Before launching a call to action—such
  as a petition, boycott, fundraising event, or demonstration—you
  should understand and be able to explain the major issue and why
  others should join the fight. People will very rarely take action
  without a good reason. Be able to explain how this action will
  help solve the problem. You don't need to tell them your entire
  campaign plan, but you should be able to provide a short paragraph explaining why the action is important, why it should occur now, and why these people should get involved.

- **Right message, right time, right people:** Think about all the messages you receive every day via email, text, Twitter, etc. And then
  think of the ones that actually make you do something. Not many,
  right? The ones that make you act typically resonate with you at a
  critical time. The message might be funny, inspirational, or sad. It
  might make you think of a childhood experience. It might reflect
  your own vision of a better world. Or it might touch a core value
  of yours. Facilitating this kind of reaction often comes down to
  the right message, at the right time, to the right people.

- **The right message:** People want to relate to other people, rather
  than to facts or figures. Craft your message in a way that allows
  your audience to make emotional and personal connections to
  your cause. You might tell them a story that vividly *shows* how
  your group or organization made a difference in someone's life
  or is solving a serious political problem. You can also make your
  supporters (rather than your group or organization) the heroes
  of the story. Explain how their time, effort, or donation will bring
  about a specific solution or ameliorate a social ill.

- **The right time:** Folks want to know why they should act now,
  at this time. In other words, people must feel the *urgency of the
  moment.* Don't overdo it, because that can backfire—being too
  extreme or fanatical can turn people off. But stressing the urgency
  of action (and the consequences of not acting) can be very effective. When appropriate, connect your issue/request/action to

something in the news. Understanding how issues come and go in the news cycle is very helpful. It may seem strange, but many serious and ongoing issues—such as pollution, immigration, hunger, homelessness, and military spending—have a short media life. At the time, it seems like the world finally gets it; your issue has the attention of the public, politicians, and the media. But then the issue falls off the radar in six months. You thus need to be ready to act in the moment and use the national (or local) attention to your fullest advantage. And this is when social media works best—send out email blasts, post Facebook comments, upload YouTube videos, and tweet away. You may not have another shot like this for quite a long time.

- **The right people:** You should rarely hit the "send all" option when sending an email or text. It's a good way to burn out fellow activists with messages that they probably don't care about. Every time you communicate via social media, you have a great opportunity to engage folks. But there's also the chance that people might decide to unsubscribe from your email list, ignore you, or lose interest in your campaign. The average email unsubscribe rate for a typical organization is about 20 percent per year. You can significantly reduce that number by segmenting your list. If possible (and if you're using email metrics), send emails to people based on their interests, activity level, location, donation history, etc. Ideally your email will be organized into different categories (people who take action, people who donate, people who volunteer time, people who support issue X). This takes a lot of effort on your part, but it makes sending the right message to the right people at the right time easier and more effective.

Developing Social Media Content

Great content is the key to social media, and that content needs to be quick, catchy, and accessible. When you write for an online medium, the message should be to the point and capable of capturing someone's interest in a few seconds. Online writing is usually fast, personal, and conversational. Great content should influence your readers to care about the issue, inspire them to take action, and motivate them to share with their networks. Below are five tips for creating brief, catchy, and accessible social media content.

1. **Engage people:** Ask conversational questions to engage your audience (as if it's a first date and you're trying to gain the person's attention and interest). When's the first time you became interested in issue X? What is your first experience with activism? Why do you support this cause?

2. **Provide basic facts:** People love short lists of the latest news. The next time you see a newsstand, check out how many magazines have a title like "Top 10 Reasons Why Celebrity X Dumped Celebrity Y." Also think about how many people discuss such top 10 lists with their friends. Now find a way to do this with your political issue: Top 10 corporate abuses of last year. Top 10 reasons to go vegan. Top 10 reasons to boycott Shell Oil. And it doesn't have to be 10—top five or top three can also work.

3. **State the relevance:** Connect your issue to what's relevant to your readers *and* to what's happening in the world. Connect the dots for them—it makes for a quicker read. Example: biking to work just one day a week significantly reduces greenhouse gas emissions.

4. **Keep it brief:** Create bite-sized pieces so readers can digest *and* share in the time it would take to read a paragraph of information.

5. **Be social:** No matter how brief the communication, a narrative voice always comes through and affects the reader. Therefore, be personable and friendly—your narrative voice should be a personality that others *want* to read.

Growing Your Activist Network

While there are countless stories of that lucky person who posted an outrageous video and now has millions of followers, most people aren't that fortunate. Instead, you must build your networks and coalitions with the magic combination of smart organizing and smart tools. In general, you need to reach thousands of people to leverage an online, grassroots presence. This may seem overwhelming, but it's very doable.

One reason why viral messages spread so quickly is because humans influence one another. We are not as independent and unique as we think. If we find out one of our friends likes something, then we are far more likely to support it, too. Shifts in public opinion are most often *not* influenced by hard facts, thought leaders, or charismatic individuals. Instead, opinions are often influenced by a critical mass of "easily influenced" individuals.[4] Peer pressure isn't limited to junior high and high school. We pretty much do what our friends are doing, and nowadays we learn about their preferences and behaviors through social media. Most people don't trust advertisers and would rather have a friend recommend a cause to join, an event to attend, or a nonprofit to donate to.

PEER-TO-PEER connections are **ESSENTIAL** for spreading your message of **SOCIAL CHANGE.**

Below are 10 guidelines for expanding your networks, building your coalitions, and, more generally, getting your word out.

1. **Content *must* be shareable:** First, use tools that allow your readers to easily share your message. Social networking sites like Facebook and Twitter are key. Second, make sure that your messages are easily shareable—keep messages brief, to the point, and catchy. And third, most people love images and short videos—these take less effort to absorb (no reading, no fuss).

2. **Find your messengers:** A small number of people are usually responsible for spreading content. Find out who these people are and get to know them. Are they influencers in their professions, communities, and networks? What motivates them to spread the word? Most people want to look good, and for many folks it's about being smart, funny, or the first one to post something. As with any favor, make sure to thank them for sharing your message, and be sure to share their messages when appropriate.

3. **Know where your supporters hang out:** What social media sites do your existing and potential supporters use? Spend some time

crafting a media plan for the networks that the majority of your supporters use.

4. **The Golden Rule:** Commenting on others' posts, tweets, or blogs is a great way to engage folks. Be sure to position yourself as a *friendly* authority on the issue as each relationship unfolds. And comment as you would want someone to comment on your posting—be respectful, humble, and considerate.

5. **Use an existing event:** While this isn't something you can always plan for, be aware of events or news that you can ride. Develop a rapid-response plan to hop on the moment. For example, in 2012 the Komen Foundation announced it would cut funding for the Planned Parenthood organization but then quickly reversed its decision due to public backlash. This gave a slew of women's organizations an opportunity to flood social media outlets with their individual (but related) messages.

6. **Cross-promote with like-minded people:** This isn't the same as just swapping supporter and/or email lists. Instead, you agree with other groups, organizations, campaigns, and/or movements to send a message on their behalf. And, of course, they send out a message on your behalf. Such cross-promotion usually happens around calls to action—you both have events occurring in the next month, for instance. The purpose is to help expand one another's networks and cross-promote one another's events.

7. **Engage targeted networks:** Sheer numbers are powerful, but finding the right people who are excited about your mission is *more* powerful. Develop a manageable list of niche groups you'd like to engage. For example, there are tons of peace action groups nationwide. With just a little research, you should be able to find viable partnerships. Know when a partnership has run its course, and don't feel committed to a group if it's not working.

8. **Like and follow:** Like and follow people on social networking sites. Start with the people you actually know in real life, and then move on to the people you'd like to know, who are interested in your cause. Make sure you are the helpful friend who also "likes" what they do and provides useful comments. This, in turn, opens

up your potential network contacts. Keep in mind that this is no small task because of the time and effort that goes into maintaining these online relationships.

9. **Use a list-building service:** If you are a well-established organization with a solid budget, then you might think about paying a company to expand your email list. Such companies send out targeted messages on your behalf. This allows *their* supporters/clients to opt in and thus receive future communications from *your* organization. (Change.org is worth noting, since it specializes in progressive causes.) Realize, though, that this approach is not the same as purchasing an email list, which is typically ineffective.

10. **Paid ads:** If you have the money, many groups have found success with targeted Facebook or Google ads. The key is to purchase the right keywords and develop an effective landing page that inspires strangers to take action. In doing so, people grant you their contact information, which can be used for future protests, events, and campaigns.

Real Example: How Left Action Grew to 500K

John Hlinko is an author and the founder of Left Action—an activist network of over one million progressives, including more than five hundred thousand fans of its flagship Facebook page.[5] When asked how he grew his supporter base as a one-person show, Hlinko said the following:

> How did Left Action grow? Actually, the story is pretty interesting and amusing. Initially, the Left Action network started to grow before Left Action itself actually existed. In April 2009, I was playing around with Facebook and doing some experimenting. I noticed that, at the time, when you became a fan of a page, it would be announced in your feed, "John Hlinko just became a fan of Starbucks/McDonalds/etc."
>
> I thought it would be amusing to have some fun with this, so I created a page called, "Not Having George Bush as President." Sure enough, when I became a fan of it, my feed

proudly announced, "John Hlinko just became a fan of Not Having George Bush as President." Well, other people apparently found it amusing as well, as the number of "fans" quickly grew into the hundreds of thousands. I followed up with other pages, such as "Telling Dick Cheney to Shut the Hell Up" and "Telling Sarah Palin She's Full of Crap." Those, too, quickly climbed into the hundreds of thousands.

It was only then that I followed up with the straightforward approach, i.e., a Facebook page named "Left Action." My reasoning was simple: although people had been drawn to the previous pages by the humor and snarky attitude, it was also clear that they were overwhelmingly Democratically-inclined activist types. Thus, when I followed up with an announcement of Left Action as the newest page—a page devoted to progressive activism opportunities—tens and then hundreds of thousands of them became fans of that page as well.

I firmly believe that if I had launched the straightforward page first, it would have gotten lost in the din of dozens or hundreds of similar-sounding lefty activist pages. But by *starting with a more creative, quirky, and noticeable approach, I was able to gain attention, and thus more effectively reach the people I ultimately wanted to reach.*

Hlinko's anecdote is a great success story—his online network went from nothing to hundreds of thousands. This is what most activists and organizers are striving for. But remember what I said at the beginning of the chapter: social change is more complicated than just posting things on Facebook. Getting people to "like" your page is not the same as mobilizing people to actually *do* something. You want people to write letters, make phone calls, lobby congress, participate in protests, boycott companies, attend speaking events and, more generally, to *put ideas into action.* Social media is a great tool that helps you do that.

PART 5

INSTITUTIONAL
CHANGE

9

The Laws and Lawyers of Social Change

DARA LOVITZ

*The problem with lawyer jokes
is that lawyers don't think they're funny
and no one else thinks they're jokes.*

— UNKNOWN AUTHOR

I WOULD BE A MILLIONAIRE IF I HAD A NICKEL FOR EVERY lawyer joke that I have heard. But if I had a nickel for every lawyer joke that I have actually found to be funny, then I would be in the same financial status that I am in now. In fact, I find jokes that mock lawyers so unfunny that I dedicated my entire law school graduation speech to those jokes. That speech argued that we—the next generation of lawyers—had to improve our negative reputation and that efforts in the pro bono ("for the public good") arena would help us beautify our collective image as a profession and regain respect in the eyes of the world.

Love Them or Hate Them, the World Needs Lawyers

Whether you laugh at lawyer jokes or find them unfunny, you cannot deny that our world needs lawyers. Our society is governed by a system of laws. Generally, lawyers work within that system to enable

173

citizens to obtain justice. As long as we have laws, we need lawyers You may not need a lawyer in every instance that involves a law or transaction, but the moment a boilerplate contract is thrown in front of you for your signature and there's a huge consequence to your decision to sign the contract, you may really appreciate the eyes of a trained professional to ensure that your rights will be met.

ACTIVISTS often target laws for SOCIAL CHANGE. Which laws are unjust and must be changed or, conversely, which laws need to be enacted in order to create a more JUST WORLD?

Some Great World-Changing Cases

Mahatma Gandhi has been credited with saying that we should be the change that we wish to see in the world. We can start to make the world a better place by understanding who we are as individuals and how we might best serve our communities. This insight no doubt applies to law and lawyers. Throughout history, lawyers have heeded the call to make important social and legal changes. Peace and social justice are lofty goals, and many lawyers have fought hard battles to further those goals. Below is a list of eight cases, in chronological order, that marked important historical turning points that substantially contributed to a more peaceful and socially just society.

Brown v. Board of Education (1954). In the United States' not-too-distant and horribly ugly past, black students could not attend the same schools as white students. Schools were segregated by race, and such segregation was deemed at the time to be constitutionally acceptable because they were considered "separate but equal." Black students filed suit against the Board of Education and others to obtain admission to the white schools, claiming that "separate" can never be "equal." Separating the races, they argued, serves to impose a sense of inferiority among the black students, which can have a negative effect on a child's motivation and ability to learn. When that segregation is sanctioned by the law, the impact is even more deleterious—there is a clear hindrance on the educational and mental development of black students. The United States Supreme Court agreed with the black students, finding that "separate educational facilities are inherently unequal" and in violation of the Due Process clause of the Fourteenth Amendment. Schools thus were desegregated, as ordered by law.

Keyishian v. Board of Regents of the University of the State of New York (1967). Harry Keyishian, among other faculty members at the University of the State of New York, was given a certificate to sign stating that he was not a communist, and that if he had ever been a communist, he had communicated that fact to the president of the university. These university employees were told that they would be dismissed if they refused to sign the certificate. In fact, Keyishian's employment contract was not renewed after he refused to sign the certificate. Keyishian and some of his colleagues brought an action against the university, claiming that the state program requiring them to sign the certificate was unconstitutional.

The United States Supreme Court found that our nation is committed to safeguarding academic freedom, which is of value to every citizen, not just teachers. Classrooms should be a safe place for the marketplace of ideas, and the university's regulation "cast a pall of orthodoxy over the classroom." The court thus agreed with Keyishian and his colleagues and invalidated the university's regulations. It quoted a prior opinion in stating,

> No one should underestimate the vital role in a democracy that is played by those who guide and train our youth.... To impose any straitjacket upon the intellectual leaders in our colleges and universities would imperil the future of our Nation.... Scholarship cannot flourish in an atmosphere of suspicion and distrust. Teachers and students must always remain free to inquire, to study and to evaluate, to gain new maturity and understanding; otherwise our civilization will stagnate and die.

Loving v. Virginia (1967). Prior to the ruling in this case, the State of Virginia had an anti-miscegenation statute that prohibited marriage between a white person and a black person. Virginians Mildred

Jeter, a black woman, and Richard Loving, a white man, traveled to Washington, DC, to marry and then returned to their home state of Virginia. They were soon arrested and charged with violating Virginia's ban on interracial marriages and sentenced to one year in prison. That imprisonment would be suspended for 25 years, however, if the couple moved out of Virginia and did not return together during that 25 years. The trial judge stated,

> Almighty God created the races white, black, yellow, malay and red, and he placed them on separate continents. And but for the interference with his arrangement there would be no cause for such marriages. The fact that he separated the races shows that he did not intend for the races to mix.

The Lovings filed suit against the State of Virginia, claiming that the anti-miscegenation statute was unconstitutional. The US Supreme Court agreed that the statute was unconstitutional in that it violated the Equal Protection clause of the Fourteenth Amendment. Although the races are treated equally in the statute in the sense that whites are forbidden from marrying blacks as blacks are prohibited from marrying whites, the court found that any statute "which makes the color of a person's skin the test of whether his conduct is a criminal offense" has no conceivable legislative purpose. The Supreme Court thus reversed the Lovings' convictions.

Phillips v. Martin Marietta Corporation (1971). Ida Phillips submitted an application for employment for the position of Assembly Trainee with the Martin Marietta Corporation. At the time of her application, a Martin Marietta employee told her that female applicants with "preschool-age children" were not being considered for the position. However, male applicants with preschool-age children were being considered. Phillips filed suit against Martin Marietta for violation of her rights to be free from gender discrimination under the Civil Rights Act. The US Supreme Court found the choice to have different hiring rules for a person based on one's gender is a violation of the Civil Rights Act.

Cohen v. California (1971). Paul Cohen was wearing a jacket with the words "Fuck the Draft" (in reference to the Vietnam War draft) in a corridor of the Los Angeles County Courthouse. He was arrested and convicted under a law that prohibited offensive conduct and disturbing the peace. He was sentenced to 30 days' imprisonment. Cohen sued, arguing his constitutional rights to free speech were violated. He argued that it was the words on his jacket that were deemed offensive, and thus the issue surrounded his speech. The prosecution argued that his act of wearing that jacket was not speech, but "offensive conduct," which was defined as behavior that had a tendency to provoke others toward acts of violence. The prosecution concluded that the words "Fuck the Draft" would reasonably cause others to feel angered enough to commit an act of violence. The prosecution also argued that Cohen's "distasteful" anti-war sentiments were "thrust upon unwilling or unsuspecting viewers" and that the arrest was to "protect the sensitive from otherwise unavoidable exposure to [Cohen's] crude form of protest."

The United States Supreme Court found that it was Cohen's speech, not his conduct, which was being punished. The Court found that the "conduct" that was ostensibly being punished was simply communication of a political message. Anyone offended by the words on his jacket can merely look away. The "offensiveness" is not imposed on anyone unwillingly. Anyone can choose, as it were, not to listen to the speech. The Court concluded that Cohen's free speech rights were thus violated, and his conviction was reversed.

Wallace v. Jaffree (1985). In this case, Ishmael Jaffree, a parent of three children who attended public school in Alabama, filed suit on his children's behalf against the school board, school officials, the governor of Alabama, and various state officials. He was claiming that his children's First Amendment rights were violated due to regular religious prayer services and other forms of religious observance in the Mobile County public schools. The prayer services included such prayers as, "Our Father, which art in heaven, hallowed be Thy name. Thy kingdom come. Thy will be done on earth as it is in heaven..." and "God is good. God is great...." Trial evidence revealed that whenever Jaffree's children stayed silent during these prayers, they were ostracized by their peers.

School prayer was endorsed by the Alabama State Legislature with statutes that authorized a one-minute period of silence in public schools "for meditation or voluntary prayer." The statues also stated that the teacher in a public school who recognizes "that the Lord God is one," at the beginning of any class, may pray or "may lead the willing students" in the following prayer to God:

> Almighty God, You alone are our God. We acknowledge You as the Creator and Supreme Judge of the world. May Your justice, Your truth, and Your peace abound this day in the hearts of our countrymen, in the counsels of our government, in the sanctity of our homes and in the classrooms of our schools in the name of our Lord. Amen.

What's wrong with religious prayer in public schools? It's unconstitutional. The First Amendment of the United States Constitution declares that Congress shall make no law respecting an establishment of religion or prohibiting the free exercise thereof. The more important part of that amendment for this case is the first part, which has been interpreted to mean, among other things, that the government may not endorse a religion because such endorsement inhibits a citizen's right to practice a different religion or no religion at all. When a government office or representative establishes a religious practice, it restricts a citizen's freedom of thought, spirituality, and reason. The US Supreme Court found that the Alabama statutes were unconstitutional because they violated First Amendment rights to freedom of religion.

Atkins v. Virginia (2002). In 1996, Daryl Atkins and William Jones allegedly abducted Eric Nesbitt, robbed him of the money on his person, drove him in his pickup truck to an automated teller machine, where cameras recorded their withdrawal of additional cash, then took him to an isolated location where he was shot eight times and killed.

During the criminal trial for Atkins, Jones and Atkins both tes-
tified and confirmed most of the details in the other's account of the
incident with one major exception: each of them stated that the other
actually shot and killed Nesbitt. Jones's testimony was more coher-
ent and credible than Atkins' testimony, and it was thus given more
weight. Atkins was convicted of abduction, armed robbery, and capital murder, and sentenced to death. Jones pled guilty to first-degree
murder, as part of a plea deal in exchange for his testimony against
Atkins. As a result of the plea deal, Jones was not subject to the death
penalty.

During the penalty phase of Atkins' trial, his defense attorney
presented testimony from a forensic psychologist who had evaluated
Atkins, interviewed people who knew Atkins, and reviewed school
and court records, including a standard IQ test resulting in a score
of 59. The psychologist gave his professional opinion based on all of
this information that Atkins was "mildly mentally retarded." Atkins'
attorney argued that Atkins could not be sentenced to death because
of his mental retardation. The attorney's argument was based on the
Eighth Amendment of the US Constitution, which prohibits "excessive" penalties and punishments. In order to determine what's excessive, the courts look to objective factors that determine our society's
standards of decency and progress.

In determining whether sentencing a mentally retarded man to
death for his crime constitutes excessive punishment, the Supreme
Court looked to other states, finding that very few ever subjected
mentally retarded individuals to the death penalty, which led it to
conclude that "it is fair to say that a national consensus has developed
against it." The Court found,

> [Mentally retarded individuals] have diminished capacities to
> understand and process information, to communicate, to ab-
> stract from mistakes and learn from experience, to engage in
> logical reasoning, to control impulses, and to understand the
> reactions of others. There is no evidence that they are more
> likely to engage in criminal conduct than others, but there is
> abundant evidence that they often act on impulse rather than

pursuant to a premeditated plan, and that in group settings they are followers rather than leaders. Their deficiencies do not warrant an exemption from criminal sanctions, but they do diminish their personal culpability.

The Court thus found that mentally retarded defendants do not have the same capacity as other defendants to understand the proceedings fully, to work with their counsel and testify in ways that would be helpful to their defense, or even to appear remorseful about their crimes, which would assist in earning jury sympathy. In other words, mentally retarded defendants are at a significant disadvantage in defending themselves. The Supreme Court concluded that a mentally retarded defendant may not be sentenced to death.

Lawrence v. Texas (2003). In responding to a neighbor's complaint, Houston police officers entered John Lawrence's home and found him engaging in a private, consensual sexual act with another man, named Tyron Garner. Lawrence and Garner were arrested and convicted of deviate sexual intercourse in violation of a Texas statute which stated,

> A person commits an offense if he engages in deviate sexual intercourse with another individual of the same sex.... ["Deviate sexual intercourse" is] any contact between any part of the genitals of one person and the mouth or anus of another person; or the penetration of the genitals or the anus of another person with an object.

Lawrence and Garner challenged the constitutionality of that statute, arguing that it violated the Equal Protection clause in the Fourteenth Amendment of the US Constitution, and that because the Texas statute was unconstitutional, their convictions under the statute should be overturned.

The Supreme Court agreed with Lawrence and Garner, finding that "when homosexual conduct is made criminal by the law of the State, that declaration in and of itself is an invitation to subject homosexual persons to discrimination both in the public and in the private spheres" and that "the Texas statute furthers no legitimate state interest which can justify its intrusion into the personal and private life of the individual." Lawrence and Garner's convictions were thus overturned.

Types of Law Jobs That Can Help You Change the World

The above case summaries illustrate that our society can be changed and presumably improved by lawyers who fight social injustices on behalf of their clients. While not every type of law job will enable you to change the world, many will. Below are some employment opportunities for lawyers looking to making a difference.

Work for a Government Office

First, the negative: working for a government office can be frustrating. Government employees complain of having to deal with a lot of bureaucracy, politics, and red tape. One cannot always "do the right thing" because there can be a whole host of political or logistical reasons not to. Also, the pay is not going to help you pay off your law school loans in any reasonable amount of time, and salaries are typically capped at a certain point, which makes working in these offices long-term a difficult decision to make.

But now the positive: you can do a lot of good. You can serve your state and the citizens who live there. You can serve as a prosecutor (also known as a district attorney) and ensure that violent individuals are stopped from further harming others, and you can ask the court to give each defendant an opportunity for rehabilitation, whether it's a drug rehabilitation process or a community service obligation. You can instead serve on the other side of the criminal procedural trial and become a public defender, appointed by the state to represent criminal defendants who cannot otherwise afford an attorney. The purpose of public defenders is thus to ensure that all accused defendants are delivered their right to a fair trial.

Government jobs can also include working for the federal government. Some examples include the Equal Employment Opportunity

Commission, where you can enforce laws against employment discrimination; the Federal Trade Commission, where you can prosecute food manufacturers who falsely advertise their products; the National Park Service, where you can protect our country's nature parks; and the Environmental Protection Agency, where you can be involved in policy decisions that attempt to improve the nation's air, land, and water quality.

Work as a Criminal Defense Lawyer

Working as a criminal defense lawyer will put you in touch with people who may have made really bad choices and may even have caused serious harm to others. But as a democratic principle, the US Constitution mandates that everyone deserves a fair trial. You, as a criminal defense lawyer, would be helping these people obtain that fair trial. Some individuals are accused of heinous crimes when they are in fact innocent—they just happened to be in the wrong place at the wrong time. Those people need a savvy lawyer to show helpful evidence to dispute the charges and exonerate them. Whereas a public defender is appointed and paid by the government, a private criminal defense lawyer is retained and paid by the defendant.

This job will also connect you with very moral people who, by way of civil disobedience, may have broken the law. A person who stages a sit-in at City Hall, for instance, may be arrested for the nonviolent act of asserting his or her rights to free speech and refusing to move upon the police officer's request. This person will need legal defense. You may also be hired to represent a person who violated trespass and property laws when endeavoring to rescue suffering animals from a factory farm—s/he will need legal representation if arrested and charged with a crime.

Work for a Nonprofit Organization

There are countless nonprofit organizations that strive to make the world a better place. They need lawyers to help draft legislation in furtherance of the cause or to file lawsuits to try to create "good law" for the issue. Not all nonprofit organizations have enough income to support a full-time lawyer, but there are a good number of larger nonprofit organizations that do employ at least one. Some lawyers help fight assaults on the environment, some help immigrants obtain rights, some help animals, etc. Name a cause, and there's most likely a nonprofit organization dedicated to it, and needing a lawyer.

Work for a Private Law Firm

You can work for a private law firm and still make quite a difference in this world. Some private law firms do world-changing and/or policy-changing work, such as suing a pharmaceutical company for failing to disclose serious health risks associated with its top-selling drugs, or suing a food manufacturer for failing to take appropriate measures to reduce the risk of food-borne illnesses.

It's hard to **FIGHT** for peace and **JUSTICE** without knowledge of laws and public policies. You may not aspire to a career in law, but activists must **UNDERSTAND** how the law works and how lawyers can help their causes.

Still, some private law firm jobs will involve the protection of assets of private individuals or corporations—not that the work is necessarily negative, but it just doesn't have the saving-the-world appeal of some other types of work. But, even if those cases make up the bulk of your work, you can still make a huge and positive impact on the world. While your full-time job will be doing what your firm hired you to do—e.g., mergers and acquisitions, taxation, estate planning, personal injury—you can still engage in world-changing work. Most private law firms either have mandatory pro bono programs or are favorable to attorneys participating in pro bono matters, as long as the attorneys' paid work is completed in a timely manner. Working for a private law firm has many perks in this regard: private firms generally have the resources to support a diligent case workup and the press contacts to bring publicity to the issue, which is helpful to the cause.

Furthering Social Justice, Finding Peace

Whichever type of law you choose, there is something inherently peaceful about fighting for social justice. Even legal battles that are lost can have a huge benefit to society. At the very least, the legal battle itself could garner a lot of free publicity that educates the public about a certain issue. Educating the public can have far-reaching implications in changing the world.

Consider the example of the animal advocacy group that files a lawsuit for animal cruelty against a foie gras producer, arguing that the very method of producing the product (shoving pipes down ducks' throats and force-feeding them until their livers expand to 10 times the natural size) violates the animal cruelty laws. The lawsuit is not likely to succeed, because most state animal cruelty codes exempt common farming practices, under which foie gras production would likely fall. But the lawsuit might be worthwhile even though chances of winning the legal battle are extremely low. The advocates could issue press releases about the suit and invite the press to attend various phases of the trial. The moment a newspaper or journal covers the issue, the animal advocates have won a small victory. Now the information typically hidden by the animal agriculture industry is out there in the public domain. People who wouldn't otherwise know how foie gras is produced are now aware. They may choose to forego foie gras, and they may choose to talk to others about what they learned. The more individuals who learn about the cruelty inherent in the production, the more likely that consumer demand for the product will diminish. At some point, reduced demand may prove to be so detrimental that an economic decision will be made to cease foie gras production altogether.

As can be seen, there's a lot of good that can come from lawyers who choose to change the world. In order to fight the good fight, however, lawyers need the support and respect of the social members that they represent. Peace and social justice are more attainable when both lawyers and citizens *work together*. Then, as a collection of different people working from different positions and angles, we can truly be "the change we want to see."

The Courage to Teach Critically: Anti-Oppression and Pro-Justice Dialogues in the Classroom

RITA VERMA

The classroom remains the most radical space of possibility in the academy. For years it has been a place where education has been undermined by teachers and students alike, who seek to use it as a platform for opportunistic concerns rather than as a place to learn. Urging all of us to open our minds and hearts so that we can know beyond the boundaries of what is acceptable, so that we can think and rethink, so that we can create new visions, I celebrate teaching that enables transgressions— a movement against and beyond boundaries. It is that movement which makes education the practice of freedom.

—bell hooks

HUMAN RIGHTS? RACE, CLASS, AND GENDER EQUALITY? Islamophobia and homophobia? Apathy? Uneasiness? Peace and justice? Oppression and liberation? Speak from your heart and your history, put yourself in someone else's shoes, break out of your comfort zone, and imagine how things might be different. These hot-button issues create uncomfortable silences, yet they should create opportunities to be embraced rather than avoided by teachers and students alike. The fear of controversy, backlash, or resistance from disgruntled parents and administrators leads many educators to shy away from doing things differently, away from teaching critically and confronting the controversial issues that face our communities, schools, and students. Ailing conditions of schools, reduced funding for education, and the anti-teacher discourse coming from the political right can hinder one's ability to teach and learn for social change. It is thus common for teachers to follow the set curriculum because it is comfortable and nonthreatening and, for the most part, "easy." Little interrogation takes place of the ideas, facts, and values that are being disseminated. The internal cultures that develop within schools are usually ignored and not discussed. The act of teaching becomes a mundane task. A moment to think about voices that are oppressed and those who are doing the oppression becomes too taxing on available time, as the pressure of mandatory testing prevails. Sparking little controversy, facts are presented, biased or Eurocentric as they may be, and we provide our students with mechanical lessons—read, repeat, review, regurgitate, and then on to the next chapter or section. The role of the educator is reduced to presenting the prescriptive curricula, and the role of the student is reduced to absorbing material and taking a test.

Through our lack of critical intervention, we in essence become advocates of the knowledge and culture that is determined by the textbook, and we strip away opportunities to ask "Why?" What are the real lessons here? A message is perhaps sent that we give more weight to half-truths, untruths, and/or fabrications, and turn away opportunities to unearth multiple perspectives and to teach *life* lessons. Critical education theorist Michael Apple challenges educators everywhere to persist in the difficult and often painful work of critically and honestly exploring the ideological assumptions and understandings that shape their work, and to confront how they themselves are implicated in the reproduction and maintenance of the dominant structure and organization of schooling.[1]

In this chapter, I share many important insights that I have gained as an educator in public school and university classrooms. There exist many examples of teachers who have the courage to teach critically and who have taken ownership of the classroom. These educators and their students are agents of change and remind us to be visionaries of a different world. This chapter presents teachable moments from the classroom where profound inquiry was required, initiatives were envisioned, and teaching objectives became exercises in self-reflection and self-empowerment. I fully understand that not everyone who reads this book is or will be a teacher. But working for justice is a systemic effort, and reforming our systems of teaching and learning is essential to creating a better world. The following narratives of self-reflective practice, pro-justice dialogues, and anti-oppression pedagogies are thus presented in a way that everyone can learn from. The basic point is to spark interrogation of your own educational experience and to understand how and why education can and should be an agent of social change.

The Larger Framework: From Hegemony to Self-Reflection

Neither schools nor the knowledge and curriculum that they present are neutral. Instead, different forms of power are exerted by our culture, the mass media, the government, familial structures, and dominant historical narratives. That is to say, a certain kind of hegemonic power exerts itself over the educational process. In brief, hegemony is the domination of one particular ideology/discourse at the expense of all others. An ideology or discourse becomes hegemonic when it excludes and represses all others. As this occurs, we become numb to its effects; it is so naturalized that we do not even think to question it. This is definitely the case with the United States educational system. For instance, it is "common sense" to adhere to romanticized notions of a Eurocentric education that is undergirded by particular values, beliefs, knowledges, and cultural forms. But we must ask ourselves, who is included and excluded within this hegemonic construction of knowledge and education? In other words, who is and who is *not* represented and valued in textbooks, lectures, curricula, and classroom discussions?[2]

Unfortunately, education has been a principal site for the reproduction and elaboration of racial meaning and racial identities. For example, after the events of September 11, 2001, discussions in schools tended to center around the "attacks" on American soil by certain "enemies." America was indeed attacked, and there were recognizable alleged perpetrators (al-Qaeda). But the "enemies" were portrayed by images of men in turbans with beards and dark skin. The issue I am addressing is not necessarily the accuracy of these images—the perpetrators may or may not have actually looked like this. Instead, my concern is how this image became the poster child for "the enemy" and how, consequently, anyone and everyone who resembles this image is assumed to be bad and evil. There was no interrogation of this image at the level of national discussion (e.g., by the White House or mass media). And, if there is no interrogation in the classroom, which is presumably a space of learning and critical reflection, then there is little hope for achieving an appreciation and love (broadly conceived) for other people who fall into the demographic of that image—i.e., Middle Eastern and Arab.

Cycles of oppression are left unbroken when there is little attempt to unlearn or dissect racist language and assumptions about groups. The groups that are negatively affected face similar tensions within school walls as they experience in the public space and outside community. These messages directly impact students' self-understanding. Issues of self-esteem and "fitting in" are critical in the formation of cultural identity and feelings of belonging for students. Lisa Bauer, in summarizing the work of Sonia Nieto, states,

> Curriculums in many United States schools today are perceived by students as being irrelevant to their lives and experiences. As a result, these students become disengaged from school. Nieto suggests educators need to examine the "hidden curriculum" reflected in bulletin boards, extracurricular activities, and other messages given to students about their abilities and talents. She notes that such practices as tracking

[i.e., separating students according to academic ability] can be problematic, and that teachers should consider [instead] what practices work well with the cultures of the students they teach.[3]

These complex social processes have become sites of struggle in schools, and new incidents of harassment and violence are cause for concern. Painting a more accurate picture of what is happening in the world and understanding the complexity of issues such as terrorism, immigration, and cultural difference are integral to achieving a more critical, reflective, and socially just educational system. What is taught in the classroom can have a positive effect in interrupting stereotypes and assumptions about race, ethnicity, gender, economic class, and so on. Yet the limited resources and prescriptive curriculum of most schools require educators to be creative in engaging students in such discussions. Values, cultural forms, and traditional knowledge that originate from Eurocentric perspectives form "core knowledge" and create limitations in curriculum. The celebration of this "core knowledge" also excludes the voices and experiences of many newly immigrated communities. Cameron McCarthy, in *The Uses of Culture: Education and the Limits of Ethnic Affiliation*, states that the representations of under-developed countries in textbooks draw on a media language that saturates popular culture both in and outside of school.[4] For example, readings and lessons on the Middle East and South Asia are often excluded from, or form a minimal part of, the curriculum. Moreover, there is a significant failure to disrupt emerging stereotypes. Islamophobia, defined as an irrational fear of or prejudice toward Muslims, is rarely disrupted, due to lack of interest on the part of educators. With the absence of an informative curriculum about the factual histories of peoples of the Middle East and South Asia, Sikh and South-Asian students (especially those who wear turbans), as well as Arab Americans, in many ways become forced to "teach" fellow students about their ethnic backgrounds.

It is important to encourage students to search for facts, challenge their own assumptions, and envision what a positive, more hopeful world would look like. The practice of "critical literacy" challenges the status quo in an effort to discover alternative paths for self- and social development. This kind of literacy connects the political and the personal, the public and the private, the global and the local, and the economic and the pedagogical. In brief, critical literacy helps us rethink our lives and enables us to promote justice rather than inequity. Critical literacy, then, is an attitude toward history, as Kenneth Burke[5] has said, or a dream of a new society against the power now in power, as Paulo Freire[6] proposed, or an insurrection of subjugated knowledges, as stated by Michel Foucault,[7] or a counter-hegemonic structure of feeling, as Raymond Williams[8] theorized, or a multicultural resistance invented on the borders of crossing identities, as Gloria Anzaldúa[9] imagined, or language used against fitting unexceptionably into the status quo, as Adrienne Rich[10] declared.

Addressing student fears and encouraging them to think about ways to engage in global understanding are also central rudiments of critical pedagogy. What is required is teacher initiative to promote discussions on issues of prejudice and stereotyping and to encourage media analysis and awareness. Educators themselves need a greater awareness of the world and need to be sensitive to their own biases and assumptions. The key point that punctuates the dialogue in my classes is the need to start from within and become self-reflective about the things we say and do. A serious engagement in self-reflection in teacher preparation is so critical to the arguments that are being developed here. Teaching for social justice, peace, and human rights requires careful analysis, thought, and determination. In the section below I share some highlights of how I encourage my students to seek out that self-reflective journey.

Self-Reflective Journeys

As a faculty member who trains future teachers (i.e., pre-service educators), I find myself situated in a key site to instigate the journey of critical self-reflection for future educators. Self-reflective practice is a critical building block for teachers as they embark on their careers as pedagogues. Being able to understand how one's practice is embedded within social, political, and cultural contexts is an initial step toward reflective action. Maxine Greene refers to this type of reflectiveness as a practice of "wide-awakeness." As she states, "Without the ability to think about yourself, to reflect on your life, there's really no awareness, no consciousness. Consciousness doesn't come automatically; it comes through being alive, awake, curious, and often furious."[11] In others words, to be fully engaged in the world, we must critically reflect.

For instance, on the first day of the semester, I ask my class of future teachers why they chose teaching as their field of study. Students often respond with something like, "I teach because I love all children," "Teaching is my calling," and/ or "I want to make a difference and touch the lives of children."

These are admirable responses, but I ask them, would they teach in a predominantly minority student school? An urban area? Do they love *all* children? The ones who are disruptive and challenging? The child who never takes notes, never completes homework, and talks in class? Do they love the student who tells them that they are wrong? Such questions are often followed by an uncomfortable silence and then some responses: "Well, I guess it will be difficult for me teach in a setting where students are different from me, or where I cannot relate to their experience," or "I think teaching should be neutral," or "I don't want to teach in a rough neighborhood." I remind my students that they are being trained to teach in all schools, urban and suburban, diverse and homogeneous, and that teacher training requires a profound and personal journey within oneself. With all due respect to my students, I embrace their fears and begin to ask them to probe further and to seek why they feel certain ways.

Their training as teachers should ultimately require that they focus on their pedagogy as inquisitive, anti-racist, anti-oppressive, and critical; and, most of all, that they should seek to create a positive learning environment and experience for *all* of their students. My students are reminded that teaching demands more of them than the simple mechanical output of information. Teaching ideally should encourage incredible interchange of ideas and knowledge production as they aim to create an atmosphere of trust, respect, openness, and hope.

In my teacher training classes, issues such as immigration, English-only policies, standardized testing, patriotism, the Pledge of Allegiance, and assimilation to United States culture become vital to address. These and similar issues are important as teachers-in-training begin comparing historical and contemporary debates and examining progress that has been made in the US system of schooling. These debates require them to reveal many of their own viewpoints about various topics. Such issues are often taught through dialogue that is situated in their life experiences in conjunction with theoretical frameworks and philosophical lenses. Such a pedagogical strategy often encourages students to take control of the debates and to learn from one another. This is not to ignore the fact that inflammatory comments are made in my classes. For instance, a former law enforcement professional who was seeking to become an educator once said that "foreigners are ruining our country. Don't fly your flag—you should fly only the American flag if you are in this country." A chemistry education student griped that "the good kids come from the good neighborhoods and those tend to be white." And a math educator told me that "low-income minority kids don't want to be in school, and their parents don't care."

These comments are obviously laden with prejudice, ignorance, and assumptions about schools, communities, and the children who attend them. I invite such discussion and do not allow these types of comments to silence the room; rather, I continue to support deconstruction of these notions and try to work with my students to reach a more balanced perspective. If educators themselves embrace ideas that are oppressive, it serves as another barrier in their ability to reach students. If teacher trainers do not unearth such ideas and negative thinking, then they also contribute to the broken system that we work in. Before educators set foot in the classroom, opportunities need to be created to engage them and require them to experience a diverse array of opinions and perspectives. Being "uncomfortable" can lead to many productive and affirmative discussions. Education based on principles of anti-oppression inevitably invites such interactions. Kevin Kumashiro, Director of the Center for Anti-Oppressive Education, provides a good summary of this process,

> Learning needs to involve challenging the idea that common-sense ways of thinking about the world—among students and among educators—are the right ways of thinking about the world. Furthermore, given the recognition that critiquing one's own worldview can be an uncomfortable process, learning needs to involve opportunities to acknowledge and work through the resistances and emotions involved in raising awareness.[12]

Sonia Nieto broadens this perspective, essentially arguing that critical pedagogy must include dialogues that connect the micro (personal experience) and the macro (systemic issues). She states,

> Educational reform cannot be envisioned without taking into account both micro- and macro-level issues that may affect student learning. Micro-level issues include the cultures, languages, and experiences of students and their families, and how these are taken into account in determining school policies and practices. Macro-level issues include the racial, social class and gender stratification that helps maintain inequality and the resources and access to learning that are provided or denied by schools.[13]

I believe that my students do come to seriously analyze the various issues involved with personal learning and the overall schooling system. They engage in many written exercises about their own schooling history. These guided visualizations of positive and negative experiences lead to a deeper understanding of the failures and successes of the system. Becoming a proponent of multicultural education, in the transformative sense, is one of the key revelations that I observe in my students. What I call for in my work is a transformative paradigm, where serious thought and analysis is given to multiple spheres of the school community and curriculum.

Multicultural education has been interpreted and developed in many different ways. "Multicultural" practices have for the most part been superficial attempts to include token holidays and heroes without a true deconstruction of curriculum and pedagogy. Educators who are committed to multicultural education with an anti-oppression perspective need to closely examine both school policies and the attitudes of the staff to determine how these might be complicitous in causing academic failure.[14] The end result can be transformative. For instance, a student of mine once came away from one of my courses with the following thoughts: "Teaching students about human rights and peace and ways that they can strengthen both gives students a sense of agency. To me, empowerment is one of the highest goals and greatest areas of potential for social studies education." These are the kinds of insights that make the uncomfortable discussions and analyses worthwhile.

Art, Reflection, and Anti-Racist Dialogue

Art, visual imagery, and political cartoons can be used as powerful pedagogical tools. An example of this is a middle school teacher of Language Arts who created a lesson plan to discuss and interrogate stereotypes. These lessons were taught throughout the year to facilitate a year-long commitment and dialogue. She teaches in a public school in a small homogeneous community in New York. Eighth-grade students were given a political cartoon that addressed issues of culture and religion, particularly the typical American confusion over Islam and Sikhism.[15] The exercise was not related directly to the class content, but was intended to provide a lesson on stereotypical perceptions and prejudices. Students spoke honestly and expressed that they might have said or thought things similar to those stated in the cartoon.

Might these honest responses offend people? Were the students being racist and oppressive? Did they have deep-seated (though unfounded) fears of certain groups, communities, and populations? Most likely, these students had never been provided the opportunity to verbalize their thoughts and were now exploring their own assumptions in a critical manner. The teacher and her class trod in deep waters and began asking the obvious questions about stereotyping, labeling, and judging. Controversies sparked, and the ugly head of prejudice faced the entire classroom.

But the class eventually moved toward other questions, such as "Who is an American?" "Who are our neighbors?" and "Don't we all look different to someone?"

The teacher then showed another cartoon. This time the main character was wearing a baseball cap. Students began to laugh and say, "Doesn't everyone know that a baseball cap is just an ordinary hat?" The connections began to be made. Students were then asked to think about an incident where they were judged incorrectly and to actually draw themselves similarly to the cartoon and to provide questions that they felt were offensive. This experiential learning exercise required the students to think about their own uneasiness and how a young man in a turban (or another traditionally non-American-identified adornment) might feel. Students came to understand that the cartoon represented apathy and ignorance and that learning about someone's culture or asking meaningful and respectful questions can generate empathy and mutual understanding. This exercise also led to issues of language and framing, with the students analyzing the questions that were portrayed in the cartoon. Are there more respectful ways to ask similar questions? If you look at the cartoon that you have drawn of yourself, what might be a more thoughtful way for someone to approach you? This generated alterative framings for the original cartoon. "How do you tie your turban on?" "Is it similar to any cap that I might wear?" "Why do you wear it?" "Does it have a specific significance?"

The political cartoon instigated a conversation that was then taken to a variety of levels as the class conducted a lesson on turban knowledge and Islamophobia. An emotional chord was struck with many of the students when they learned that 80 percent of Sikh youth in Queens, New York, are harassed on a daily basis. (Queens is close to the location where this class occurred.) Although images of Osama bin Laden and the Taliban may not appear on American television every evening as they did in the early 2000s, those images (and the codifications thereof) have become part of American "common sense." Those images have become ingrained in the immediate memories of the general public and have created a racialized stigma that continues to be used to target communities with hatred and violence.

Students also engaged in a discussion about racial epithets and the language they used to depict groups of people. Despite the offensiveness of some of the cartoons that the teacher showed in class, this exercise enabled students to begin sharing the personal details of their own experiences with stereotypes and racism. The teacher also shared her personal experiences, which led to a powerful exchange and acted as a bridge for group understanding. African American students turned the discussion to the racism that they had experienced, focusing on the need to educate people on their history and the experience of being judged because of their skin color. Jewish students spoke about the Holocaust, the tragedies their ancestors had faced, and the religious discrimination they encountered. There were also one Muslim and two South-Asian students who shared their experiences. The Muslim girl mentioned a raid that took place at her uncle's house for no apparent reason. The South-Asian students spoke about a Sikh parade that took place in Queens, where onlookers threw garbage at the Sikh families. Students also shared examples of what was commonly occurring in schools between different racial groups. In the middle school, students grouped themselves according to their racial background. And at the high school, there had been violent outbreaks between the black and white students. These discussions, although difficult and intense, allowed the students to empathize with one another and to become individuals with unique backgrounds rather than abstract stereotypes. Such pro-justice and anti-oppression teaching can be healing, joyful, and visionary.

It should be noted, too, that the teacher often encouraged her students to use art to express their own cultural identities. Visual representations of self can provide powerful lessons and open up a safe space for students to share how they define themselves and the personal struggles they may face. The process of developing the artistic work is coupled with reflective essays and larger group discussions that ultimately become affirming and celebratory interactions. Shown are two samples of student artwork on visual self-representation—one from a South-Asian female representing her struggles with bicultural identity formation, the other from a Sikh male reflecting upon the American flag.

Language and Anti-Oppression

An unfortunate, though common, statement in the classroom might look something like this: "Arabs are all terrorists. I would never learn their language. Why would I?" Such comments are offensive and inappropriate for many reasons. But like many of the examples above, these comments can be used as a springboard for discussion, reflection, and growth. This is especially true for courses that are focused on language—e.g., world languages, foreign languages, literature, rhetoric, and composition.

With the presence of Islamophobia in today's schools and curriculum, language educators can play important roles in linking the words we speak to the Arabic language. Islamophobia has extended to numerous social arenas, including but not limited to news media, popular culture, politics, college bullying, and job discrimination. Learning about the Arabic language—and its connections to Western languages—provides opportunities for students to evaluate their potential biases toward and fears of the Islamic "other." Learning that many of the words that we speak are rooted in Arabic origins can be a powerful teaching moment.

You can begin by having students explore the origin of English, Spanish, and French languages. Most people don't realize that numerous words from these languages can be traced back to Arabic. After Latin and English, Arabic is probably the biggest contributor of words to the Spanish language, and a large portion of English-Spanish cognates that don't come from Latin come from Arabic. For example, the English word *magazine* and the French word *magasin* come from the Spanish *almacén* and the Arabic *al-makhzan*, both of which mean *storehouse*. The English word *sofa* and the Spanish word *sofá* come from *suffa*, which is Turkish and Arabic for *rug* or *divan*. *Algebra* is Arabic for *the reduction* and came into European languages as part of the title of an Arab mathematical treatise.

INVESTIGATING the etymological origins of words can reveal the **CONNECTIONS** between peoples and **CULTURES.**

Such etymological exercises ask students to reflect upon the ways in which languages are intimately tied to one another—with the added emphasis that *we as people* are also tied to one another not just by languages, but by histories, cultures, and transmigrations. Learning to appreciate these interconnections gives students an opportunity to relate to other languages, cultures, and peoples in more positive and mutually confirming ways. If you have the right conditions and resources, it is also helpful to have students meet with native speakers from other countries and/or cultures and work with those speakers on collaborative and/or service learning projects. This direct communication can lead to friendships, provide a human touch to the language experience, and allow students to see and relate to the world through the words and ideas of others.

Final Thoughts on Fighting the Wider Fight

Not everyone who reads this desires to be a teacher. But, presumably, most or all of us have been students and have therefore been affected, either positively or negatively, by years of schooling and education.

This provides a rallying point for shared values and collective action, for joining together in demanding a more inclusive curriculum and a better, more humane educational system that places anti-oppression at the center of the learning experience. As Michael Apple and James Beane state,

> Those committed to a more participatory curriculum understand that knowledge is socially constructed, that it is produced and disseminated by people who have particular values, interests and biases. This is simply a fact of life, since all of us are formed by our cultures, genders, geographies and so on. In a democratic curriculum, however, young people learn to be "critical readers" of their society. When confronted with some knowledge or viewpoint, they are encouraged to ask questions like: Who said this? Why did they say it? Why should we believe this? and Who benefits if we believe this and act upon it?[16]

Likewise, Paulo Freire states,

> One of the most important tasks of critical educational practice is to make possible the conditions in which learners, in their interaction with one another and with their teachers, engage in the experience of assuming themselves as social, historical, thinking, communicating, transformative, creative persons: dreamers of possible utopias, capable of being angry because of a capacity to love.[17]

Teachers who dare to think outside of the box and to teach in critical, uncomfortable, and self-reflective ways enable education to be liberatory and learning to be transformative. If we are serious about creating a more just and peaceful world, then we must also be serious about education, schooling, teaching, and learning.

Thankfulness, Mutual Recognition, and Appreciation

KIM SOCHA AND ANTHONY J. NOCELLA II

> *The smallest act of kindness is worth more than the grandest intention.*
>
> — OSCAR WILDE

THE WORLD CAN OFTEN BE COLD, INDIFFERENT, AND UNCARing. That is actually one reason why activists do what they do—to create a warmer and more supportive world. But, ironically, activists can also fall victim to uncaring attitudes. Perhaps you are working on a new campaign with a large group of people whom you barely know. You are familiar with the names and faces, but do not really know anyone on a personal basis. On top of that, you are working day and night with little rest or sleep. Those deadlines are fast approaching, and you're dedicating more time and effort than you had planned. Although you believe in the cause, you feel under-appreciated. This feeling of under-appreciation permeates everything you do. You still go to the meetings, help out, and accomplish your tasks, but you do so reluctantly. You feel like you don't matter, like your efforts go unnoticed. If this is true for you, then it's probably also true for other folks who are working on the project. But how does a group break out of this negative spiral?

Sometimes simply saying "thank you" can be enough. We all work hard, and we all want to change the world. But sometimes we can get so wrapped up in completing the immediate task that we forget to acknowledge the people standing right next to us. Whether we want to admit it or not, this is a form of emotional neglect that perpetuates some of the social ills that we are trying to change. This can be avoided by simply *expressing* some appreciation to one another. Literally tell others how much you appreciate their work and effort. Say things like: thank you, you're welcome, please, nice job, great effort, you are doing a great job, we couldn't do this without you, I appreciate all the work you are doing, this project is better with you on board, you are making this a much better campaign. Such small gestures can go a long way in making people feel wanted, acknowledged, appreciated, supported, and affirmed. It is safe to assume that this is what *every* person wants. If that's true, then we shouldn't hesitate to recognize and appreciate one another's efforts.

"Thank you" and "please" are phrases taught to children when they are given something nice or someone does something for them or says something positive about them. Thank-you letters and goodwill messages date back hundreds of years in the Eastern and African cultures to express one's gratitude. "Thank you" and "please" are humbling expressions to appreciate others, and they argue for a social morality through an exchange of services and/or respect.

The following are some ways to show appreciation to those within your activist community:

- **Informal get-togethers:** These allow people to get to know each other in more relaxed settings. Such get-togethers might include potluck dinners, happy hours, dance parties, festivals, going to the movies, inviting people over to watch a documentary about the issue you are working on, taking "field trips" to amusement parks or the beach, etc. The whole point is to build community and facilitate non-stressful conversation and interaction; people are then more likely to connect on a personal level.
- **Written acknowledgements:** These can be inserted into books, manuscripts, magazines and zines, newspapers, community newsletters, flyers, posters, event programs, etc.

- **Oral acknowledgements:** These can be announced before, during, and at the end of meetings and strategizing sessions.
- **Social media acknowledgments:** These can be done via Twitter, Facebook, emails, blogs, or websites. You might say things like "Thanks for the talk the other night!" or "Great job the other day!" You might also use the person's name, as in "Jane Doe led a great workshop yesterday! Can't wait until she comes back again!"
- **Photos, videos, and audio recordings:** These can give people a sense of recognition and can be easily uploaded and shared through social media.
- **Awards and certificates:** These can be formal "end of the year" ceremony awards or informal "do it yourself" arts and crafts. Regardless, the point is to acknowledge and congratulate the efforts of hardworking interns or assistants, helpful volunteers, and others for their work on outstanding books, good articles, impressive research projects, well-done rallies and demonstrations, good speeches, acts of heroism, artistic contributions, etc. (Award and certificate templates are easily findable online.)
- **Private handwritten notes:** These can be person to person, from a single person to a group of people, or even from a large group to one person. These can be handwritten on pieces of paper or store-bought "thank you" cards. Regardless of the form, it's always good to hand write some kind of brief note and sign your own name. That kind of personal touch communicates greater affection and appreciation. The same kind of gesture can also be accomplished through emails; however, the time and effort of an actual handwritten note communicates more care and intimacy.
- **Sponsors and co-sponsors:** Most events are sponsored, hosted, and/or organized by multiple groups and organizations. Always acknowledge everyone involved in making an event happen, from adding them to an event program flyer or mentioning them verbally at the beginning and/or the end of the event. Depending on the space limitations, that recognition might be by individual name or by the group/organizational name.
- **Brief thank yous before or after talks/workshops:** It's always nice for speakers and facilitators to thank the audience members for

attending and the organizers for creating the event; likewise, it's nice for the audience to thank the speakers/facilitators and organizers.

- **Texts and phone calls:** These are probably best after some big project—a rally, march, conference, forum, public panel, etc. Thank the folks who helped out, and let them know that you sincerely appreciate all that they did.

The sincerity of your appreciation should be kept in mind. Saying thank you should not be another task to be checked off of your to-do list. Instead, it should come from the heart. Take a moment to actually think about what the person has done and why that effort is important. Then, from that emotional place, speak offhand or write down your appreciation. That moment of private reflection can mean the difference between a sincere thank you and a superficial gesture.

While we live in the era of the nonprofit industrial complex in the West, where everyone is paid for their acts of kindness, we must remember that not all of us are compensated financially. Publically and/or privately appreciating someone's time, financial contributions, and energy helps build friendships rather than the business partnerships of the nonprofit world. Volunteers get involved in social justice because they care about others and their environments. Therefore, we must respect each others' abilities to support a given movement, and not engage in comparisons of who cares more or guilt someone into doing work for which one does not feel able. We will truly understand what it means to give affirmation when we can understand and be humbled by the idea that we are not owed anything by each other. When you give thanks, do not expect anything in return, but be gracious when your appreciation is reciprocated.

Also realize that different cultures and populations have different ways of showing appreciation and will thank different kinds of efforts. For instance, some indigenous populations might be more likely to thank and acknowledge the natural environment, nonhuman species, and/or world spirit(s). This kind of recognition breaks down barriers between human and nonhuman worlds, thus fostering a more ecologically balanced way of life. Further, if you are working with individuals who do not speak the native language of the country in which you organize, learn how to say "thank you" in their original language. There are websites that not only provide phrasing, but verbal pronunciations as well. This sensitivity to others' cultures is sorely missing in industrialized societies. These are examples of how thanks and appreciation can directly extend one's politics.

Speaking of politics, we must also consider our various forms of cultural privilege and power when engaged in activism of any sort. Any movement plagued by hierarchy and oppression within its intimate structures will not be effective if it perpetuates the very problems it purports to challenge. A prime example of this dynamic is found within the animal rights and liberation movements, though it most certainly manifests everywhere. While the vast majority of such activists are female-identified persons, the leadership and theoretical voice (with notable exceptions) is predominately male and heteronormative. Thus, stories arise of women feeling ignored, discarded, and exploited therein.

Male appreciation of female work within a movement, whether offered privately or publically, can reinforce patriarchal relations if not attended to with tact—i.e., it can sometimes come off as condescending or patronizing. One must truly reflect upon the privileges of one's gender and actively work to overcome that privilege, even with something as simple as saying "thanks." Further, sometimes those folks working "behind the scenes" of a given cause do not want public recognition because of their cultural, political, or personal beliefs, which may also relate back to gender. In that case, thanking can be a sign of disrespect, and it is important to first ask those with whom you organize how they feel about public recognition. Always respect their decisions and fight any urges to change their minds.

There is a further tendency in justice movements for those with the loudest voices or the highest academic degrees to garner credit for successful social organizing events. Indeed, the media will often seek out sound-bites from organizers with "PhD" after their names and/or those already well-established in a community. At these times, the best way to show appreciation is to give the microphone to someone else—to that person or those people who have been "in the trenches" fighting oppression without ever being asked to speak to their work and of the cause(s) for which they fight.

Issues of race are also of great import within social justice movements. Again using animal advocacy as an example, the movement is overwhelmingly populated by white-identified individuals (again with notable exceptions), and activists of all genders must be constantly aware of their racial and/or financial privilege and supremacy before they attempt to speak to other communities about what they *should* be consuming and wearing. For instance, on feminspire. com, a website dedicated to female issues and authors, Briana Ureña-Ravelo wrote a piece entitled "Why White Feminists Need to Shut Up and Listen When It Comes to Race." While the title may sound harsh, Ureña-Ravelo identifies one of the most effective things activists can do, especially when attempting to become allies with diverse communities: be quiet and listen. For example, if you are a white woman subjugated by patriarchy or a white man with disabilities stymied by ableism, do not assume you understand the oppression of a man that is Black in America or a teenage girl from Pakistan. Rather, you should listen to those stories of systemic and violent racism and sexism and refrain from using the disingenuous response, "I understand." You do not understand, but that doesn't mean you cannot be that person's friend and ally—*if* they are open to it.

There is wonderful scene in Spike Lee's *Malcolm X* (1992) in which a young blonde woman approaches Malcolm and asks what she can do for the cause of Black liberation. He responds that there is nothing she can do and summarily walks away from the dumbfounded aspiring activist. Later in the movie, Malcolm has a change of heart when he travels to Mecca and finds himself in the presence of white individuals with whom he feels kinship. The point of this story is to be cognizant of why your desire to help may not fit the needs of an individual or group at a certain moment in time. And as difficult as it is to accept, sometimes the best thing you can do is to step away. In the meantime, there is always other work to do to challenge oppression and hierarchy in its many forms. If we are not aware of these intricate dynamics of gender, race, and class, we will never even get to the point of being able to say to or hear from someone new: "Thank you for all the work you have done. I enjoy organizing with you."

But at the same time we argue for the need to appreciate others' work, we must remain aware of potential problems therein. For example, an anarchist such as David Graeber examines the history of thanking and sees it as an acknowledgement of credits and debt, which he argues promotes capitalist ideology. Quakers are also opposed to rewards, awards, and acknowledgements because they see them as elitist, supportive of power hierarchies, and inherently unnatural. That being said, to be effective in various social justice movements and cultural contexts, anarchists and Quakers *do* appreciate and thank one another in modest ways within their communities.

We must also be willing to challenge and be challenged to effect positive social change. While we are both East Coast natives, at the time of this writing, we are living in and around the Twin Cities and have come into contact with a geographical tendency known as "Minnesota Nice," which basically means people are so focused on being nice to each other that they stifle disagreement and forget that revelations can arise from challenging one another's ideas and ideologies. Conflict, while it can be destructive, also leads to opportunity in the right situations. In our drive to be grateful to our comrades, we forget that questioning strategies and viewpoints allows for growth of individuals and movements. As activists, therefore, we find it imperative to critique each other, from the terminology we use, to the assumptions we make, to how we behave toward each other and other activists. Admittedly, such interactions have not always been fun or easy, but while challenges and criticism may not feel comfortable in the moment, we realize they ultimately make us feel appreciated that someone cares enough to want us to develop as individuals and advocates. Therefore, do not discount the power of kindly worded critiques as a way of showing others you respect, recognize, and appreciate them. These kinds of instructions on how and why to show thanks and appreciation are often absent from organizing and activist manuals. This is understandable since such gestures are usually taken for granted. But we believe that showing thanks is another strategy for social change. Building a better world starts with the smallest of gestures that then ripple out into the universe. Acknowledging one another's efforts may not sound as exciting as taking on corrupt legislators or battling world capitalism, but it is essential to promoting peace and justice. It is in that spirit that we thank you, the reader, for everything you have done—and for everything you *will* do—in the name of social change.

Resources for Peace and Justice Activists

The following sources are intended to aid and further develop your work for peace and justice. This list is by no means exhaustive, but rather an introduction to material covered in this book.

Manuals and How-To Books

Alinsky, Saul. *Rules for Radicals: A Pragmatic Primer for Realistic Radicals.* New York: Vintage Books, 1971/1989.

Brown, Michael Jacoby. *Building Powerful Community Organizations: A Personal Guide to Creating Groups that Can Solve Problems and Change the World.* Arlington, MA: Long Haul Press, 2006.

Choudry, Aziz, Jill Hanley, and Eric Shragge, eds. *Organize!: Building from the Local for Global Justice.* Oakland, CA: PM Press, 2012.

Cooney, Nick. *Change of Heart: What Psychology Can Teach Us About Spreading Social Change.* New York: Lantern Books, 2011.

Cutting, Hunter and Makani Themba-Nixon. *Talking the Walk: A Communications Guide for Racial Justice.* Oakland, CA: AK Press, 2006.

Del Gandio, Jason. *Rhetoric for Radicals: A Handbook for 21st Century Activists.* Gabriola, BC: New Society Publishers, 2008.

Kaufman, Cynthia. *Ideas for Action: Relevant Theory for Radical Change.* Cambridge, MA: South End Press, 2003.

Lakoff, George. *Don't Think of an Elephant: Know Your Values and Frame the Debate: The Essential Guide for Progressives.* White River Junction, VT: Chelsea Green Publishing Company, 2004.

Lasn, Kalle. *Culture Jam: How to Reverse America's Suicidal Consumer Binge—and Why We Must.* New York: Quill, 2000.

Kush, Christopher. *The One-Hour Activist.* San Francisco, CA: Jossey-Bass, 2004.

Mann, Eric. *Playbook for Progressives: 16 Qualities of the Successful Organizer.* Boston, MA: Beacon Press, 2011.

Minieri, Joan, and Paul Getsos. *Tools for Radical Democracy: How to Organize for Power in Your Community.* San Francisco, CA: Jossey-Bass, 2007.

Reinsborough, Patrick, and Doyle Canning. *Re:Imagining Change: How to Use Story-Based Strategy to Win Campaigns, Build Movements, and Change the World*. Oakland, CA: PM Press, 2010.

Salzman, Jason. *Making the News: A Guide for Activists and Nonprofits*. Boulder, CO: Westview Press, 2003.

Shaw, Randy. *The Activist's Handbook: A Primer*. Berkeley, CA: California University Press, 2001.

Solnit, David, ed., *Globalize Liberation: How to Uproot the System and Build a Better World*. San Francisco, CA: City Lights Books, 2004.

Zuniga, Markos Moulitsas. *Taking on the System: Rules for Radical Change in a Digital Era*. New York: Celebra, 2008.

Anthologies, Encyclopedias, and Overviews

Button, John. *The Radicalism Handbook: Radical Activists, Groups and Movements of the Twentieth Century*. London, UK: Cassell, 1995.

Cieri, Marie, and Claire Peeps, eds., *Activists Speak Out*. New York: Palgrave, 2000.

Duncombe, Stephen, ed., *Cultural Resistance Reader*. New York: Verso, 2002.

Kahn, Seth, and Jonghwa A. Lee, eds., *Activism and Rhetoric: Theories and Contexts for Political Engagement*. New York: Routledge, 2011.

MacArthur, Brian, ed., *The Penguin Book of Twentieth-Century Protest*. New York: Viking (of Penguin Books), 1998.

McCarthy, Timothy Patrick, and John McMillian, eds., *The Radical Reader: A Documentary History of the American Radical Tradition*. New York: The New Press, 2003.

Morris, Charles E., and Stephen Howard Brown, eds., *Readings on the Rhetoric of Social Protest*. State College, PA: Strata Publishing, 2001.

Riedner, Rachel, and Kevin Mahoney. *Democracies to Come: Rhetorical Action, Neoliberalism, and Communities of Resistance*. Lanham, MD: Lexington Books, 2008.

Sharp, Gene. *Politics of Nonviolent Action*. Boston, MA: Porter Sargent Publisher, 1973.

Stewart, Charles J., Craig Allen Smith, and Robert E. Denton, Jr., *Persuasion and Social Movements*. Long Grove, IL: Waveland Press, 2012.

Training Organizations

Academy for Peace Education: criticalanimalstudies.org/research-groups /academy-for- peace-ed

AlternateROOTS: alternateroots.org

Center for Story-Based Strategy: storybasedstrategy.org
Center for Community Change: communitychange.org
The Folk Education Association of America: peopleseducation.org
Highlander Research and Education Center: highlandercenter.org
The Midwest Academy: midwestacademy.com
National Peace Academy: nationalpeaceacademy.us
Project South: projectsouth.org
The Ruckus Society: ruckus.org
Training for Change: trainingforchange.org

Contributors' Biographies

Anniessa Antar is a social justice educator and prison abolitionist dedicated to transformative justice. She has worked with various prison abolition/prisoner justice groups, including Save the Kids, in the Twin Cities, and the Life After Life Collective, in Montreal. She also helped produce and host Prison Radio Show on CKUT in Montreal. She currently lives in Minneapolis, and is developing an alternative to the suspension program at a local high school. She enjoys karaoke and is motivated and inspired by the amazing students she works with every day.

Larry Albert Butz is an activist who has campaigned for reorientation toward environment, compassion for animals, equality and social justice, an end to corruption and secrecy in American government, and an expansion of fair trade practices in the marketplace. Since relocating to Houston in 2012, he has become secretary and student outreach coordinator for the Houston Animal Rights Team and a member of the Rice Progressives. As a PhD student in English at Rice University, Larry works in the fields of Critical Animal Studies and Bio/Zoopolitics, studying historical figurings of animality as well as posthumanism.

Melissa Chiprin is a California journalist/radio producer reporting on a range of subjects, including juvenile justice, Indigenous Peoples' rights, sex trafficking and social justice movements. She is an organizer with Los Angeles Save the Kids and producer on Pacific-Radio's Scholars' Circle, with a B.A in Women's Studies, California State University, Fullerton. Chiprin's community involvement has included mentoring targeted teenagers, leading international political campaigns to abolish sex trafficking, and peer counseling with women who are homeless and affected by alcohol and drug addiction.

Jason Del Gandio, PhD, is an Assistant Professor of Rhetoric and public Advocacy at Temple University. His areas of scholarly expertise include the philosophy of communication, social and political theory, rhetoric, and critical analysis with a focus on social movements and radical social change.

Jason has participated in the Global Justice Movement, the Anti-war movement, the anti-Republican National Committee demonstrations of 2004, fair trade campaigns, Latin American solidarity work, and the Occupy movement. Jason has appeared on television and radio, and regularly speaks on college campuses and at public venues. His first book is entitled *Rhetoric for Radicals: A Handbook for 21st Century Activists.*

JAMES GENERIC is a longtime Philadelphia activist. He has been a member of the Wooden Shoe collective for 13 years, and has been involved in a variety of organizations, campaigns, and struggles. He is a member of Philadelphia Solidarity and the founder of the Oregon Ave Octopi, a radical softball team in South Philly. James earned a master's degree in liberal arts from Temple University. He is a sportswriter focusing on the intersections between social justice and sports, such as communist-sponsored baseball and basketball teams in the 1930s–'40s.

JENNIFER GRUBBS is a doctoral student in anthropology at American University, specializing in race, gender, and social justice. She is currently a co-ordinator for the Working Group Committee on Humane Research with the Institute for Critical Animal Studies. Her past research includes an auto-ethnography of Farm Sanctuary, a Marxist-anarchist analysis of animal industries, and a feminist analysis of animal slavery. Her current research expands on the intersectionality of oppression, the animal liberation movement, and the capitalist mode of production. As a vegan anti-capitalist anarchist, she uses her academic position to queer the normative nonsense that happens in the ivory tower.

JOSHUA RYAN HOLST is a consultant, documentarian, and doctoral candidate in applied anthropology at the University of Arizona. His environmental and social justice consulting for nonprofits has taken him throughout Southeast Asia, Latin America, West Africa, and California. In the US, Joshua served on several community committees focused on voting and inequality, as well as on the boards of directors of two environmental political action committees. He has worked closely with the Anti-globalization movement, the American Indian movement, Occupy Wall Street, the Indigenous Congress of Chiapas, and the Global Environmental Justice movement.

JOY JAMES is Presidential Professor of the Humanities at Williams College and visiting scholar in African and African Diaspora Studies at the University of Texas, Austin, where she curates the Harriet Tubman Literary Circle, a digital repository on human rights. She is the editor of several critical anthologies on US democracy and political and mass incarceration: *The New Abolitionists, Imprisoned Intellectuals,* and *Warfare in the American Homeland.* Her books on feminism and race include *Shadowboxing: Representations of Black Radical Politics; Transcending the Talented Tenth: Black Leaders and American Intellectuals;* and *Resisting State Violence: Radicalism, Gender, and Race in US Culture.* James's most recent publication is *Seeking the Beloved Community: A Feminist Race Reader.*

MICHAEL LOADENTHAL is a proud father, anarchist organizer, clandestine conspirator, and academic insurgent based in Washington, DC. Over the past 15 years, he has been involved in a number of anti-authoritarian projects around the world, and presently focuses his energies on developing challenges to the State's criminalization of dissent. A doctoral fellow and on-again, off-again adjunct, Michael currently splits his time between raising a vegan daughter, researching Statecraft, teaching theory, and agitating for a better world. He regularly publishes propaganda and political theory under a variety of pseudonyms, and is the co-author of the website *Thoughts of a Pregnant Vegan.*

DARA LOVITZ authored *Muzzling A Movement: The Effects of Anti-Terrorism Law, Money, and Politics on Animal Activism.* She is Adjunct Professor of Animal Law at the law schools of Temple University and Drexel University. She was selected by *Super Lawyers Magazine* as a "Rising Star." Lovitz earned her BA, *magna cum laude,* from the University of Pennsylvania and her JD from Temple University Beasley School of Law, where she was selected by her classmates to be the graduation speaker. She is a board member of Four Feet Forward, Peace Advocacy Network, and the Equal Justice Alliance.

PETER MCLAREN is Professor of Urban Schooling at the Graduate School of Education and Information Studies, University of California, Los Angeles. He is also currently Distinguished Fellow in Critical Studies at Chapman University, California. Professor McLaren's work has been translated into 20 languages. One of his books, *Life in Schools: An Introduction to Critical Pedagogy in the Foundations of Education,* was chosen in 2004 as one of the 12 most significant education books worldwide by an international panel commissioned by the Moscow School of Social and Economic Sciences and by the Ministry of Education of the Russian Federation. The government of Venezuela recently honored Professor McLaren with the International Award in Critical Pedagogy.

ANTHONY J. NOCELLA II, PhD, award-winning author, community organizer, and educator, is Visiting Professor in the School of Education at Hamline University and Senior Fellow of the Dispute Resolution Institute at the
Hamline University School of Law. Nocella is a scholar-activist grounded in
the field of education and peace and conflict studies. His interests include
social justice education, school-to-prison pipeline, critical pedagogy, disability pedagogy, ecopedagogy, transformative justice, hip-hop pedagogy,
critical animal studies, and eco-ability. Dr. Nocella has published more than
50 scholarly articles and 15 books.

ALISHA PAGE is the editor of Wisdom Behind Walls, a project of Save the
Kids, which shares letters online and to youth from current prisoners who
provide advice on such topics as crime, incarceration, oppression, anger
management, life skills, and justice. Page became involved in prisoner support when her brother Maurece Graham was incarcerated. He is currently
in prison in Minnesota and is involved in Wisdom Behind the Walls. Page
is a life coach for signatureplanning.org, one of the founding members of
Peoples Union, a derivative of Prisoners Union. Alisha is passionate about
transformative justice, youth, and creating social change by partnering
with those who are dedicated to prisoner support and alternatives to incarceration.

JEANETTE RUSSELL has been a nonprofit leader for the last 15 years and
brings extensive knowledge of nonprofit technology, advocacy organizing,
and fundraising. She serves as Senior Partner Marketing Manager for Salsa
Labs, which provides an integrated online organizing platform to thousands
of progressive organizations. Previously, for nearly 10 years, she organized
thousands of nonprofits and activists around national forest protection. As a
pioneer for change, she currently serves on the board of the WildWest Institute and the Missoula New Leaders Council.

KIM SOCHA, PhD, Indiana University of Pennsylvania, is author of *Women,
Destruction, and the Avant-Garde: A Paradigm for Animal Liberation*
(Rodopi 2011) and is a contributing editor to *Confronting Animal Exploitation: Grassroots Essays on Liberation and Veganism* (McFarland Publishing
2013) and *Defining Critical Animal Studies: A Social Justice Approach for Liberation* (Peter Lang 2014). She has also published on topics such as Latino/a
literature, surrealism, composition pedagogy, and critical animal studies.
Her next book will look at the connections between secular thought and the
animal liberation movement. Kim is an English professor and activist for
animal liberation, drug policy reform, and transformative justice.

RITA VERMA, PhD, is Associate Professor in the School of Education at Adelphi University in New York and Director of the Peace Studies Program. Dr. Verma is the author of *Backlash: South Asian Voices on the Margins*, and editor of *Be the Change: Teacher, Activist, Global Citizen*. Her work is also featured in numerous books and scholarly journals. She has worked with the United Nations and other human rights organizations on a variety of projects.

DREW ROBERT WINTER is the director of publications at the Institute for Critical Animal Studies and a PhD student at Rice University in the Anthropology department. Named one of the "Top 20 activists under 30" by *VegNews* magazine for his leadership and organizing for nonhuman animals, he works at the grassroots level toward a holistic, intersectional approach to social justice. Winter works with many advocacy- and research-oriented groups, including Food Not Bombs, Vegan Outreach, the Animals and Society Institute, and the Humane Research Council. He also cohosted and coproduced the online show *Radical Radio*.

AARON ZELLHOEFER and his partner Kevin live with their dog Junior in Minneapolis. Upon going sober at the age of 18, Aaron changed his approach to life. He became vegan and started to work for social justice. Sixteen years later, he is still at it. He was involved in the Stop Huntingdon Animal Cruelty campaign, which saw the closure of Europe's largest contract research organization, only to have it bailed out by the British government. Aaron's partner was prosecuted by New Jersey governor Chris Christie and was imprisoned for five years for his involvement in the campaign. Aaron most recently worked on a voter amendment campaign in Minnesota.

Endnotes

Preface

1. Chris Hedges, "The Hijacking of Human Rights," Truthdig, April 7, 2013, truthdig.com/report/item/the_hijacking_of_human_rights _20130407.
2. Rob Blackhurst, "The air force men who fly drones in Afghanistan by remote control," *The Telegraph*, September 24, 2012, telegraph.co.uk /news/uknews/defence/9552547/The-air-force-men-who-fly-drones-in -Afghanistan-by-remote-control.html.
3. "User Review," Amazon, accessed October 1, 2013, amazon.com/Maisto -Fresh-Metal-Tailwinds-Endurance/product-reviews/B004JFMOGK ?pageNumber=3.

Introduction

1. Martin Luther King, Jr., "Letter from Birmingham City Jail," in *A Testament of Hope: The Essential Writings and Speeches of Martin Luther King, Jr.*, ed. James M. Washington (New York: HarperCollins Publishers, 1986), 292.
2. Carmen DeNavas-Walt, Bernadette D. Proctor, and Jessica C. Smith, *Income, poverty, and health insurance coverage in the United States: 2011*, US Census Report, September 2012, census.gov/prod/2012pubs/p60 -243.pdf .
3. Sarah Anderson, et al. "Executive Excess 2010: CEO Pay and the Great Recession," Institute for Policy Studies, accessed October 1, 2013, ips-dc .org/reports/executive_excess_2010.
4. David M. Haugen et al., eds. *Social Justice: Opposing Viewpoints Series*, (Detroit: Greenhaven Press, 2010), 15.
5. Adam Gabbatt, "2012 US campaigns have cost more than $4bn, election commission says," *The Guardian*, September 26, 2012, guardian.co.uk /world/2012/sep/26/2012-us-campaigns-cost-4bn?newsfeed=true.
6. Richard Johnson, "Mapping a Superpower-sized Military," *National Post*, October 28, 2011, news.nationalpost.com/2011/10/28/graphic -mapping-a-superpower-sized-military/.

7. Peter W. Singer, "Comparing Defense Budgets, Apples to Apples," *Time*, September 25, 2012, nation.time.com/2012/09/25/comparing -defense-budgets-apples-to-apples/.

8. Arshad Mohammed and Phil Stewart, "US says nuclear arsenal includes 5,113 warheads," *Reuters*, May 3, 2010, reuters.com/article/2010/05/03/us -nuclear- treaty-usa-arsenal-idUSTRE64251X20100503?feedType=RSS &feedName=topNews.

9. "Cosmetic and Product Testing," Humane Society of the United States, accessed October 1, 2013, humanesociety.org/issues/cosmetic_testing/.

10. "What's Wrong with Factory Farming?" Center for Food Safety, April 7, 2004, centerforfoodsafety.org/search/whats-wrong-with-factory -farming.

11. Ibid.

12. David Biello, "Oceanic Dead Zones Continue to Spread," *Scientific American*, August 15, 2008, scientificamerican.com/article.cfm?id =oceanic-dead-zones-spread.

13. Max Follmer, "Five Reasons to Brown Bag Your Lunch: A Sackful of Goodness," Take Part, January 28, 2011, takepart.com/article/2011/01 /28/five-reasons-brown-bag-your-lunch-sackful-goodness.

14. "How often does sexual assault occur?" Rape, Abuse & Incest National Network, accessed October 1, 2013, rainn.org/get-information/statistics /frequency-of-sexual-assault.

15. "11 Facts About Sweatshops," accessed October 1, 2013, dosomething .org/tipsandtools/11-facts-about-sweatshops; and "Sweatshops," ac- cessed October 1, 2013, greenamerica.org/programs/sweatshops/what toknow.cfm.

16. David Abramowitz, "It's time for anti-slavery action, Mr. President," *CNN*, January 10, 2013, thecnnfreedomproject.blogs.cnn.com/2013/01 /10/its-time-for-anti-slavery-action-mr-president/.

17. "Modern Slavery Statistics," Abolition Media, accessed October 1, 2013, abolitionmedia.org/ about-us/modern-slavery-statistics.

18. Howard Zinn, *You Can't Be Neutral on a Moving Train: A Personal His- tory of Our Times* (Boston: Beacon Press, 2002).

Chapter 1

1. Mahatma Gandhi, in Carmella B'Hahn, "Be the Change You Wish to See: An Interview with Arun Gandhi," *Reclaiming Children and Youth* 10(1) (2001): 7.

2. Martin Luther King, Jr., "The World House," in *A Testament of Hope: The Essential Writings and Speeches of Martin Luther King, Jr.*, ed. James M. Washington (New York: HarperCollins Publishers, 1986), 626.

3. "Unethical Companies," Action for Our Planet, accessed October 1, 2013, actionforourplanet.com/#/top-10-unethical-companies/4545796858.
4. nfca.coop/definition.
5. For more information, see: Paulette Stenzel's Fair Trade Institute: fairtrade-institute.org.
6. For an extended yet succinct explanation of the relationship between communication, social norms, and activism, see: Jason Del Gandio, *Rhetoric for Radicals: A Handbook for 21st Century Activists I* (Gabriola, BC: New Society Publishers, 2008), 18–23.
7. For more discussion about spreading this type of symbolic change, see: Nick Cooney, *Change of Heart: What Psychology Can Teach Us About Spreading Social Change* (New York: Lantern Books, 2011) 151–168.
8. See: Jason Del Gandio and Anthony J. Nocella II, eds., *The Terrorization of Dissent: Corporate Repression, Legal Corruption, and the Animal Enterprise Terrorism Act* (Brooklyn: Lantern Books, in press).
9. See: selected works by Judith Butler, Peggy McIntosh, Luce Irigaray, bell hooks, and many, many others.

Chapter 2

1. Saul Alinsky, *Rules for Radicals: A Pragmatic Primer for Realistic Radicals* (New York: Vintage Books, 1971/1989), (1989) 81.

Chapter 3

1. Max Weber, *Politics As a Vocation* (New York: Fortress Press, 1965/1991).
2. David Graeber, *Possibilities: Essays on Hierarchy, Rebellion, and Desire* (Oakland, CA: AK Press, 2007).
3. Robert A. Dahl, *On Democracy* (New Haven, CT: Yale University Press, 1998).
4. James C. Scott, *The Art of Not Being Governed: An Anarchist History of Upland Southeast Asia* (New Haven, CT: Yale University Press, 2009).
5. Leo Gross, "The Peace of Westphalia, 1648–1948," *American Journal of International Law* 2(1) (1948): 20–41; and Charles Tilly, "War Making and State Making as Organized Crime," in *Bringing the State Back In*, Peter B. Evans, Dietrich Rueschemeyer, and Theda Skocpol, eds. (Cambridge, UK: Cambridge University Press, 1985).
6. Jose Barreiro, ed., *Indian Roots of American Democracy* (Ithaca, NY: Cornell University Press, 1988).
7. Graeber, *Possibilities.*
8. Bruce Gilley, "Democratic enclaves in authoritarian regimes," *Democratization* 17(3) (2010): 389–415.
9. See: the work of Hakim Bey, for instance.

10. Susan Welch et al., *Understanding American Government* (Boston, MA: Wadsworth Publishing, 2010).

11. Mark Hugo Lopez, Karlo Barrios Marcelo, and Emily Hoban Kirby, "Youth Voter Turnout Increases in 2006," Center for Information & Research on Civic Learning & Engagement (Madison, WI: Tufts University, 2007).

12. Michael McDonald, United States Elections Project, accessed October 1, 2013, elections.gmu.edu.

13. Carmen DeNavas-Walt, Bernadette D. Proctor, and Jessica C. Smith, "Historical Income tables: Households," *Income, poverty, and health insurance coverage in the United States: 2011*, US Census Bureau Report, September 2012, census.gov/prod/2012pubs/p60-243.pdf .

14. Ralph Miliband, *The State in Capitalist Society* (New York: Basic Books, 1969).

15. C. Wright Mills, *The Power Elite* (New York: Oxford University Press, 1956).

16. Richard G. (Gene) Niemi, Herbert F. Weisberg, and David C. Kimball, eds., *Controversies in Voting Behavior, Fifth Edition* (New York: CQ Press, 2010).

17. Frances Fox Piven and Richard A. Cloward, *Poor People's Movements: Why They Succeed, How They Fail*, (New York: Vintage Books, 1979) 15.

18. Graeber, *Possibilities*.

19. "Civil society" is a contested term, with some scholars arguing that it applies only to the advantaged classes of society with access to politics. In practice, however the term is typically used by NGOs and government agencies to include all community organizations, especially those of the poor.

20. *Manufacturing Consent: Noam Chomsky and the Media*, directed by Mark Achbar and Peter Wintonick (1992; New York: Zeitgeist Video, 1992).

21. Edward Bernays, *Propaganda* (New York: Horace Liveright, 1928) 37.

22. Arjun Appadurai, *Fear of Small Numbers: An Essay on the Geography of Anger* (Durham, NC: Duke University Press, 2006).

23. Graeber, *Possibilities*, 341.

24. Paulo Freire, *Pedagogy of the Oppressed*, New York, Continuum, 1986.

25. Drake Bennett, "David Graeber, the Anti-Leader of Occupy Wall Street," *Businessweek*, October 26, 2011, businessweek.com/magazine/david-graeber-the-antileader-of-occupy-wall-street-10262011.html.

26. Laura Nader, "Controlling Processes: Tracing the Dynamic Components of Power," *Current Anthropology* 38(5) (1997): 711–737.

27. Ernesto Laclau and Chantal Mouffe, *Hegemony and Socialist Strategy: Towards a Radical Democratic Politics.* (London, UK: Verso, 1985).

Chapter 4

1. Parts of this chapter were first published in "Transforming Justice and Hip Hop Activism in Action," in *From Education to Incarceration: Dismantling the School to Prison Pipeline* Anthony J. Nocella II, Priya Parmar, and David Stovall, eds. (Peter Lang Publishing, forthcoming 2014).
2. "Dr. Cornel West says President Obama, Politicians are 'Cowards' for Lack of Response to Gun Violence in the Black Community," *Your Black World*, December 2012, yourblackworld.net/2012/12/black-news /dr-cornel-west-says-president-obama-politicians-are-cowards-for -lack-of-response-to-gun-violence-in-the-black-community/.
3. "The Punishing Decade: Prison and Jail Estimates at the Millennium," Justice Policy Institute, May 2000, justicepolicy.org/images/upload/00 -05_rep_punishingdecade_ac.pdf.
4. Daniel Burton-Rose, Dan Pens, and Paul Wright, eds. *The Celling of America: An Inside Look at the US Prison Industry* (Monroe, ME: Common Courage Press, 1998); and Angela Y. Davis, *Are Prisons Obsolete?* (New York: Seven Stories Press, 2003).
5. Davis, *Are Prisons Obsolete?*
6. ProCon.org, "Prostitution," prostitution.procon.org.
7. sextraffickingsurvivorsunited.org.
8. For more on sex trafficking, see: Michelle Bachelet, "Fighting Human Trafficking: Partnership and Innovation to End Violence against Women and Children," UN General Assembly Interactive Dialogue, April 3, 2012, unwomen.org/en/news/stories/2012/4/fighting-human -trafficking-partnership-and-innovation-to-end-violence-against -women-and-children; Chuck Neubauer, C. (2011, April 23). "Sex Trafficking in the U.S. Called 'Epidemic': 'No class and no child is immune,'" *The Washington Times*, April 23, 2011, washingtontimes.com /news/2011/apr/23/sex-trafficking-us-called-epidemic/?page=all#page break; and and Alexandra S. Pierce, "Shattered Hearts: The Commercial Sexual Exploitation of American Indian Women and Girls," *Minnesota Indian Women's Resource Center*, November, 2009, miwrc.org/wp -content/uploads/2013/12/Shattered-Hearts-Full.pdf.
9. For these projects, visit savethekidsgroup.org/?page_id=3803 and then scroll over "publications."
10. It is important to note that conflict-studies scholars, who are predominantly white able-bodied heterosexual men and economically well

off, often assume that conflict is nice and neat and includes a limited number of factors. But this is not always an accurate depiction of conflict from those of marginalized and/or oppressed populations. In these cases, models of conflict might include many other factors, such as: (1) intimate and interpersonal factors, (2) community and street-level factors, (3) institutional and systemic factors, (4) state and enforcement factors, and (5) ideological and structural factors. See the work of the Life after Life Collective for more information: facebook.com/lifeafter lifecollective.

11. Ron Claassen, *Options for Handling Conflict* (Fresno, CA: Center for Peacemaking and Conflict Studies, 1995).

12. Ron Claassen, "Restorative Justice—Fundamental Principles," Fresno Pacific University, May 1996, peace.fresno.edu/docs/rjprinc.html.

13. Ruth Morris, *Stories of Transformative Justice* (Toronto, CA: Canadian Scholars Press, 2000); and Donna Coker, "Transformative Justice: Anti-subordination Processes in Cases of Domestic Violence," in *Restorative Justice and Family Violence*, Heather Strang and John Braithwaite, eds. (Cambridge, UK: Cambridge University Press, 2002) 128–152.

14. Anthony J. Nocella II, "An Overview of the History and Theory of Transformative Justice," *Peace & Conflict Review* 6(1) (2012): 1–10.

15. Theda Skocpol, *Social Revolutions in the Modern World* (Cambridge, UK: Cambridge University Press, 1995).

16. Nocella, "An Overview of the History."

17. Nocella, "An Overview of the History."

Chapter 5

1. The two are certainly not mutually exclusive; there is extensive overlap, as activism helps with organizing by promoting the group and the issue, and organizers are themselves dedicated activists.

Chapter 6

1. Site discontinued. For more information see multi.lectical.net/web/site /occupy_philly_media.

2. I first heard this insight articulated by Sine from the Red Emma's Bookstore Coffeehouse collective, an anarchist bookstore in Baltimore.

3. The Wooden Shoe website (woodenshoebooks.org) has links to similar bookstores/infoshops around the country, including Red Emma's Bookstore Coffeehouse.

4. The following two interviews with Carlbom provide additional background on the MUAF campaign: Andy Lien, "Organization of the Year: An Interview with Richard Carlbom, Campaign Manager of Minneso-

tans United for All Families," *Lavender*, December 13, 2012, lavender
magazine.com/our-affairs/interview-richard-carlbom; and Brett Ste-
vens, "Politics: Talking Strategy with Richard Carlbom," *Lavender*,
February 21, 2013, lavendermagazine.com/our-affairs/talking-strategy
-with-richard-carlbom.

5. Doug Grow, "Dayton delivers 'surprises' throughout State of the State
speech," *Minnpost*, February 7, 2013, minnpost.com/politics-policy/2013
/02/dayton-delivers-surprises-throughout-state-state-speech.

6. See: Victoria Law, "Closing Cages: People Power Helps Stop Youth
Incarceration," *Truthout.org*, March 11, 2013, truth-out.org/news
/item/15023; and Campaign for Youth Justice, "Facts and Research,"
campaignforyouthjustice.org/facts-a-research.html.

7. Jared A. Ball, *I Mix What I Like!: A Mixtape Manifesto* (Oakland, CA:
AK Press, 2011).

8. Lance Williams, "Hip-hop as a Site of Public Pedagogy," in *Handbook of
Public Pedagogy: Education and Learning Beyond Schooling*, Jennifer A.
Sandlin, Brian D. Schultz, and Jake Burdick, eds. (New York: Routledge,
2010) 230.

9. Anthony J. Nocella II, "An Overview of the History and Theory of
Transformative Justice," *Peace & Conflict Review* 6(1) (2012): 1-10.

Chapter 8

1. The author would like to acknowledge that social media experts John
Hlinko and J.D. Lasica contributed to sections of this chapter.

2. Mary Madden and Kathryn Zickuhr, "65% of online adults use social
networking sites," Pew Internet & American Life Project, August 26,
2011, pewinternet.org/Reports/2011/Social-Networking-Sites.aspx.

3. google.com/nonprofits

4. Duncan J. Watts. and Peter Sheridan Dodds, "Influentials, Networks,
and Public Opinion Formation," *Journal of Consumer Research, Inc.* 34
(2007).

5. Facebook.com/LeftAction; also see: leftaction.com.

Chapter 10

1. Michael W. Apple, *Ideology and Curriculum* (New York, NY: Routledge,
2004).

2. See: Michael W. Apple, *Cultural Politics and Education* (New York:
Teachers College Press, 1996); and Michael Apple and James Beane,
"Lessons from Democratic Schools," in *Democratic Schools: Lessons in
Powerful Education, Second Edition*, Michael Apple and James Beane,
eds. (Portsmouth, NH: Heinemann, 2007) 150–156.

3. Lisa Bauer, "[Review of] Language, Culture, and Teaching: Critical Perspectives for a New Century," *TESL-EJ*, 5(4) (March 2002), tesl-ej .org/ej20/r9.html.

4. Cameron McCarthy, *The Uses of Culture: Education and the Limits of Ethnic Affiliation* (New York: Routledge 1998).

5. Kenneth Burke, *Attitudes Toward History* (Berkeley, CA: University of California Press, 1984).

6. Ira Shor and Paulo Freire, *A Pedagogy for Liberation: Dialogues on Transforming Education* (Westport, CT: Bergin & Garvey, 1987).

7. Michael Foucault, *"Society Must Be Defended": Lectures at the Collège de France 1975–1976* (New York: Picador, 2003).

8. Raymond Williams, *Marxism and Literature* (New York: Oxford University Press, 1977).

9. Gloria Anzaldúa, *Borderlands/La Frontera: The New Mestiza* (San Francisco, CA: Spinsters/Aunt Lute, 1990).

10. Adrienne Rich, *On Lies, Secrets, and Silence: Selected Prose 1966–1978* (New York: W.W. Norton & Company, 1979).

11. "Maxine Greene: The Importance of Personal Reflection," Edutopia, edutopia.org/maxine-greene-daring-dozen-2008.

12. Kevin K. Kumashiro, "Alternative Models of Learning," Center for Anti-Oppressive Education, accessed October 3, 2013, antioppressiveeduca tion.org/definition.html.

13. Sonia Nieto, *The Light in Their Eyes: Creating Multicultural Learning Communities* (New York: Teacher's College Press, 1999) 167.

14. Nieto, *The Light in Their Eyes.*

15. For examples, see: sikhtoons.com.

16. Apple and Beane, "Lessons from Democratic Schools," 151.

17. Paulo Freire, *Pedagogy of Freedom: Ethics, Democracy, and Civic Courage* (Lanham, MD: Rowman & Littlefield, 2001) 33.

Index

If you have enjoyed *Educating for Action*,
you might also enjoy other

BOOKS TO BUILD A NEW SOCIETY

Our books provide positive solutions for people who want to
make a difference. We specialize in:

Sustainable Living • Green Building • Peak Oil
Renewable Energy • Environment & Economy
Natural Building & Appropriate Technology
Progressive Leadership • Resistance and Community
Educational & Parenting Resources

New Society Publishers

ENVIRONMENTAL BENEFITS STATEMENT

New Society Publishers has chosen to produce this book on recycled
paper made with **100% post consumer waste,** processed chlorine
free, and old growth free.

For every 5,000 books printed, New Society saves the following
resources:[1]

26	Trees
2,327	Pounds of Solid Waste
2,560	Gallons of Water
3,339	Kilowatt Hours of Electricity
4,230	Pounds of Greenhouse Gases
18	Pounds of HAPs, VOCs, and AOX Combined
6	Cubic Yards of Landfill Space

[1]Environmental benefits are calculated based on research done by the
Environmental Defense Fund and other members of the Paper Task Force who study
the environmental impacts of the paper industry.

For a full list of NSP's titles, please call 1-800-567-6772 *or check out our website* at:

www.newsociety.com